The SiMS™ Vacation

EXPANSION PACK

PRIMA'S OFFICIAL STRATEGY GUIDE

DAVID CHONG

MARK COHEN

PARKWAY VILLAGE

Prima Games
A Division of Random House, Inc.

3000 Lava Ridge Court
Roseville, CA 95661
(916) 787-7000
www.primagames.com

Senior Product Manager: Jennifer Crotteau
Senior Project Editor: Christy L. Curtis

Important:

ISBN: 0-7615-3622-0

Library of Congress Catalog Card Number: 2002102494

Printed in the United States of America

02 03 04 BB 10 9 8 7 6 5 4 3 2 1

Acknowledgments

Thanks to the many people who helped make this book possible, including Jonathan Knight, Virgin McArthur, Melissa Bachman-Wood, Waylon Wilsonoff, Sean Baity, Jake Simpson, and Michael McCormick.

ontents

INTRODUCTION: HOW TO USE THIS BOOK

Introduction

The Sims is not a game, it's a phenomenon. It has no end—none of the hundreds of thousands of people playing has ever "won" the game. With an unrivalled fan following and passionate support from its creators at Maxis, *The Sims* and its expansion packs have at times held all of the top spots in the computer game sales rankings. Clearly, the game has done something right.

This guide is not just a handbook for *The Sims Vacation* expansion pack, but a thorough companion for the entire game. There's a lot to consider in *The Sims* game world, and you'll want this guide by your side as long as you are playing the game. All of the game concepts are thoroughly explained to help you get started if you're new to *The Sims*, but we've also included in-depth resources that will serve as reference aids for even the most veteran Simmers. Much of the information on these tables is exclusive, never-before released insight into the inner workings of the game, including minimum relationship scores for interaction success, personality motivations, souvenirs, vacation scoring, the hidden skill objects, and more.

Part I: The Sims

This guide is split into two parts: *The Sims* (chapters 1–9) and *The Sims Vacation* (chapters 10–13). The first part introduces the original game and is a basic primer on all of the fundamental game concepts. Experienced players will still find many valuable reference tools in this part of the guide, clearly titled for easy reference.

Chapter 1, "What's Your Sim Sign?", explains how a Sim thinks, acts, and reacts in various situations. At the beginning of the game, you can mold your Sims' basic personalities, and we tell you how these traits affect their lives.

Chapter 2, "Motives—I Want, I Need; Therefore, I Am a Sim!", explains the eight primal urges that drive all Sims. We cover each one in detail, then blend the information with the previous chapter, so that you understand how a Sim's actions can be manipulated by you, and by other Sims.

Sims are very social creatures, and this can be a blessing or a curse. Chapter 3, "Interacting with Other Sims," shows you how and why a Sim interacts with others, and explains the benefits and pitfalls that accompany friendships, love relationships, and children.

Chapter 4, "9 to 5—Climbing the Career Ladder," looks at the working life of a Sim. You have myriad career choices and opportunities for advancement, and we provide you with the tools to get the job and promotions that will make your Sim financially successful.

Chapter 5, "Building a House," takes you through every step of the construction process, from putting up the framing to slapping on the final coat of paint. Our topics include walls, windows, doors, wall coverings, stairways and second stories, pools, and landscaping.

A Sim home is empty until you fill it with lots of stuff. Chapter 6, "Material Sims," provides facts and statistics on every object you can buy, more than 150 items in all. In addition to data and descriptions, we use detailed lists and tables to show how items relate to each other, and how some objects can even alter the effectiveness of other objects.

Now, it's time to put everything you know into action. We devote chapter 7, "All in the Family," and to describing the common and not-so-common events in a Sim's life. Get ready for a wild ride as we give you insights on single life, relationships, having children, and making friends.

Chapter 8, "A Day in the Life," follows a few of our families as they handle the ups and downs of Sim life. Check it out to see examples of our Sims in interesting situations.

Chapter 9, "Sim Survival Tips," is a quick-reference guide for times of crisis. Simply turn to the appropriate Motive and save your Sim's life with one of our game-tested tips. Or, if you're feeling devious, check out our cheats to satisfy your Sim's needs.

Part II: The Sims VACATION

The Sims Vacation adds a new Vacation Island to the mix. Your Sim children benefit from expanded interactions to match the adult interactions first included in *Hot Date*. You don't have to "unlearn" any of the original game features; the differences represent *growth* instead of outright change.

Part II helps you get a handle on the new game concepts, which affect all aspects of gameplay. Furthermore, you'll learn everything there is to know about sending your Sims on a dream vacation, with strategies for building the perfect resort and keeping your Sims happy once they're there.

Chapter 10, titled "Cabin Fever," encompasses the new facets of your Sims' personalities and relationships: *The Sims* is essentially a game about these two subjects, and in *Vacation* they reach full maturity. New interaction trees, expanded interests, and new children's interactions are all part of the new social system. Plus, detailed tables present the requirements for success for each interaction in the game.

Chapter 11, "Vacation Playgrounds," looks at the new objects included in *Vacation*. Included is a buying guide to all of the new objects, as well as strategies for using the new object types.

Get the inside scoop on the features of the all-new Vacation Island in Chapter 12, "Paving Over Paradise." We explore building strategies, planning considerations, and the essential elements for all of the attractions and activities a luxury resort can offer. Additional tips help you incorporate the new building elements into your home.

Chapter 13, "Getting Away from It All" covers every aspect of taking your Sims on a successful vacation. Learn how to plan and execute a vacation itinerary, meet new Sims on the island, get your Sims underway, and take care of them while they are vacationing. Also learn about the new souvenir system and vacation score. Then you can send your Sims on the vacation of their dreams.

PART 1:

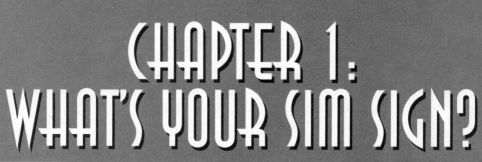

CHAPTER 1:
WHAT'S YOUR SIM SIGN?

Introduction

When you are charged with the solemn task of creating a Sim from scratch, you have 25 points to distribute over five traits: Neat, Outgoing, Active, Playful, and Nice. Whether we admit it or not, all of us have an inherent wish to be perfectly balanced people (or Sims). Of course, you can take the easy way out and award five points in every category, creating a generic Sim. You'll spend less time managing a middle-of-the-road Sim because in most situations, he or she will do the right thing. If you'd rather play it safe, skip this chapter and move right to "Motives: I Want…I Need…Therefore, I Am a Sim". If not, read on as we describe the subtle (and sometimes dramatic) outcomes that your personality ratings will inspire.

It's in the Stars

As you play with the personality bars, you'll note the changing zodiac sign that appears on the screen. Of course, a serious astrologer would argue that a true personality profile is based on much more than five traits. However, if you have a basic understanding of newspaper horoscopes, you'll be able to recognize yourself, or someone close to you, as you create a Sim personality. In the next section we'll look at each trait and examine the potential effects of your ratings in various game situations. But first, let's take a look at basic interpersonal compatibility as seen through the eyes of the zodiac. The following table gives you the best and worst matchups for friends and lovers. This doesn't necessarily imply that any other Relationship outside of the table is doomed; it is merely an indication of how hard you'll have to work on it.

Sims Zodiac Compatibility Table

SIGN	ATTRACTED TO	REPELLED BY
Aries	Gemini/Taurus	Cancer/Libra
Taurus	Aries/Libra	Virgo/Cancer
Gemini	Pisces/Virgo	Capricorn/Aries
Cancer	Taurus/Scorpio	Gemini/Aries
Virgo	Aquarius/Sagittarius	Leo/Taurus
Libra	Virgo/Cancer	Pisces/Scorpio
Scorpio	Pisces/Leo	Libra/Aquarius
Sagittarius	Pisces/Capricorn	Libra/Scorpio
Leo	Sagittarius/Cancer	Capricorn/Gemini
Capricorn	Aquarius/Taurus	Leo/Gemini
Aquarius	Capricorn/Sagittarius	Scorpio/Virgo
Pisces	Scorpio/Gemini	Leo/Aries

Personality Traits

The following sections review what you can expect from each type of Sim, with examples of how different personality traits will manifest during the game. For our purposes, we'll divide the ratings bar into three sections: Low (1–3), Average (4–7), and High (8–10). These numbers correspond to the number of light blue bars to the right of each trait.

Neat

Low

Don't expect these Sims to pick up their dirty dishes, wash their hands after using the bathroom, or take timely showers. They are perfectly content to let others clean up their messes.

Fig. 1-1. The kitchen floor is a perfect place for this messy Sim's snack leavings.

Fig. 1-3. This fastidious Sim goes straight to the bathtub after a hard day's work.

Medium

At least these Sims keep themselves relatively clean, and you can depend on them to clean up their own messes. Occasionally they'll even clean up another Sim's garbage, but you might have to intervene if you have several cleanup items that need attention.

Outgoing

Low

Shy, reserved, Sims have less pressing needs for Social interaction, so it will be more difficult to pursue friendships with other Sims, although they can still carry on stimulating conversations. Within their own home, a shy Sim may be less interested in receiving hugs, kisses, and back rubs, so if you are looking for romance, it would be a good idea to find a compatible target (see zodiac chart on p. 2).

Fig. 1-2. After slopping water all over the bathroom during his shower, this moderately neat Sim mops up his mess before leaving the room.

Fig. 1-4. This Sim cringes at the thought of a back rub—poor guy.

High

A super-neat Sim always checks the vicinity for dirty dishes and old newspapers, and of course, personal hygiene is a big priority. One of these Sims can compensate for one or two slobs in a household.

Medium

It will be a little easier to get this Sim to mix with strangers and enjoy a little intimacy from his housemates. Don't expect a party animal, but you'll be able to entice your guests into most activities.

Fig. 1-5. Come on everyone, let's hit the pool!

High

This Sim needs plenty of Social stimulation to prevent his or her Social score from plummeting. You'll have no trouble throwing parties or breaking the ice with just about any personality type.

Fig. 1-6. This outgoing Sim is still unconscious from last night's pool party, and she has inspired the close friendship of another man. Hmmm.

Active

Low

Forget about pumping iron or swimming 100 laps at 5:00 a.m. These Sims prefer a soft easy chair to a hard workout. A sofa and a good TV are high on their priority list. In fact, if they don't get their daily ration of vegging, their Comfort scores will suffer.

Fig. 1-7. This Sim says "No way!" to a session on the exercise bench.

Medium

These Sims strike a good balance between relaxing and breaking a sweat. They dance, swim, and even shoot hoops without expressing discomfort.

Fig. 1-8. His Active rating is only a four, but that doesn't stop this Sim from shooting hoops in his jammies.

High

Active Sims like to pick up the pace rather than fall asleep on the sofa in front of the TV. Get these Sims a pool, basketball hoop, or exercise bench, and plan on dancing the night away with friends.

Fig. 1-9. Even in her business suit, this active Sim will gladly leave Mortimer on the sofa and pump some iron in the backyard.

Medium

These well-rounded Sims are usually receptive to a good joke and don't mind a little tickling. They may not be the first ones on the dance floor, but they'll join in with a good crowd.

Fig. 1-11. This Sim is Playful enough to dance, even though she is overdue for a shower.

Playful

Low

Get these Sims a bookcase, a comfortable chair, and plenty of books. If reading isn't an option, looking at a painting or playing a game of chess will do just fine.

Fig. 1-10. There's always time to watch the fish, for this less-than-playful Sim.

High

Can you spell P-A-R-T-Y? These Sims love to have a few drinks, dance to good music, and invite lots of guests over to the house. They love telling jokes, and they are usually ready to laugh at others' stories.

Fig. 1-12. This Playful kid would get the Maid in the pool for a game of chicken, if only she would respond.

Nice

Low

There is nothing redeeming about a grouchy Sim. They are always ready to tease or insult their friends, and they love to brag. A Sim with a low Nice rating should be dropped from your guest list immediately, or asked to leave if he or she shows up.

Fig. 1-13. Usually a compliment elicits a nice response, but not so with with sourpuss.

Medium

This Sim keeps an even keel about most things. Of all the traits, Nice is the least destructive if you award at least four points. Only the nastiest Sims can get under a medium-Nice Sim's skin.

Fig. 1-14. This Sim has time for a good tickle, even while mopping up the bathroom.

High

These Sims just want to make the world a better place for everyone. If there was a Sim beauty contest, the winner would be extremely "Nice."

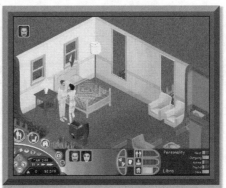

Fig. 1-15. Even after spending the night on the kitchen floor, this Sim still knows how to compliment her mate.

Personality Tables

The following tables demonstrate how personality traits affect Fun scores and Skill development.

Traits that Raise Max Fun Value

PERSONALITY TRAIT	RAISES MAX FUN SCORE FOR
Playful	Aquarium, Chess Table, Computer, Doll House, Flamingo, Pinball, TV (Cartoon Channel), VR Glasses
Serious (Low Playful)	Newspaper (Read)
Active	Basketball Hoop, Play Structure, TV (Action Channel)
Outgoing	Hot Tub, TV (Romance Channel)
Grouchy (Low Nice)	TV (Horror Channel)

Skills Accelerated by Personality

SKILL	OBJECTS USED TO INCREASE SKILL	TRAIT ACCELERATOR
Creativity	Easel, Piano	Playful
Body	Exercise Machine, Swimming Pool	Active
Charisma	Medicine Cabinet, Mirrors	Outgoing

CHAPTER 2:
MOTIVES—I WANT, I NEED;
THEREFORE, I AM A SIM!

Introduction

When you consider how many needs, traits, and desires make up a Sim's personality, it would be an injustice to call it AI. Never before has a computer-generated character interacted so completely with both the game and the gamer while maintaining a unique (and ever-changing) personality. Is it any wonder that *The Sims* has topped the PC sales chart for nearly two years running?

In the previous chapter we discussed a Sim's personality traits. It painted a broad picture of the various types of Sims you might encounter in the game, much the same as a newspaper horoscope tells a superficial story of a person's life. In this chapter, we advance from broad-brush personality traits to the eight powerful Motives that drive a Sim's every action. We cover each Motive in detail, but first, let's begin with a few basic definitions.

What Is a Motive?

A Motive is, very simply, a need. Your Sims follow these needs, based on their own instincts and a little help from you. If you activate Free Will in the Options menu, your Sims will also make their own decisions, based on changing needs. After selecting a Motive to fulfill, be it Hunger or Hygiene, the Sim is "rewarded" with Motive points. These points raise the corresponding Motive score.

The eight Motive scores are displayed on the right side of the control panel. A Motive rating is considered positive if the bar is green, and negative if it is red. Internally, the game uses a 200-point system, with positive (green) ratings between 0 and 100, and negative (red) ratings from 0 to -100.

TIP
When any of the Sims' eight Motives drop below a certain level, a Sim will cease an activity that doesn't improve the Motive in distress. So, you'll see low-priority items drop out of the activity queue, or your Sim will add an activity that addresses the critical need.

CAUTION

Without Free Will, your Sims depend entirely on your input to keep them alive. If you don't tell them to eat, they will starve, and eventually die.

Mood Rating

The game control panel also displays a Mood Rating, just to the right of the Sim character icons. If the rating is positive, you see up to five green bars displayed above the comedy/tragedy masks. When the Mood Rating is negative, it displays up to five red bars below the masks.

In calculating the Mood Rating, each of the eight Motives is weighted, based on how critical it is to sustaining a Sim's life. Hence, Hunger, Bladder, and Energy, which are all related to a Sim's physical well-being, carry more weight than the noncritical Motives such as Social, Fun, or Room. So, if a Sim is hungry and tired, as pictured in figure 2-1, the overall Mood Rating will be relatively low, even if several other Motives are high.

Fig. 2-1. This Sim kid's overall Mood Rating is barely positive, due to the fact that he is starving and low on Energy.

The Motives

In the following sections we describe the eight Motives, using several tables to show you how and why a Sim reacts to different objects in the environment. By recognizing the relationships between Motives and objects, you'll begin to understand how a Sim considers a perpetual barrage of options. Once you do this, the only remaining question is, "Who is really in charge here, you or the Sim?"

Fig. 2-2. This Sim family enjoys a meal together. Mom's Hunger bar is in the worst shape, so she has a second meal plate at the ready.

NOTE

Aside from the overall Motive weighting system, each Sim suffers different rates of Motive depreciation based on personality traits. For example, a Playful Sim must have more "rewards" to maintain the Fun Motive bar. Similarly, an Outgoing Sim requires more interaction with other Sims to maintain the Social score.

Hunger Score for Each Meal, Snack, or Gift

MEAL TYPE	HUNGER MOTIVE BAR POINTS
Snack	9
Quick Meal	16
Full Meal	16
Group Meal (per serving)	16
Pizza (per serving)	33
Candy Box (gift)	3 (per serving, 12 servings per box)
Fruitcake (gift)	7 (per slice, 6 slices per box)

Hunger

For obvious reasons, a Sim cannot survive for very long without food. We'll cover the details of food preparation in a later chapter, but for now let's focus on the basics. As long as you have a refrigerator, a Sim can enjoy a Snack, Quick Meal, Full Meal, or Group Meal (same as a Full Meal, except one of the Sims prepares several servings). In addition to preparing food, a Sim with a telephone can order out for Pizza, or enjoy food that was brought as a gift (Candy Box or Fruitcake). The Hunger Motive bar points awarded with each meal are outlined in the following table.

Comfort

The next category listed in the Needs section of the control panel is considerably less important than Hunger. Sims like to be comfortable, and they love cushy chairs, oversized sofas, and supportive beds. Spending more money on these objects translates into greater Motive rewards. However, if your budget is tight, you must still furnish the house with basic furniture or your Sims will express their discomfort.

Fig. 2-3. With only a cheap chair and loveseat, this Sim's Comfort score is mired in the red.

Fig. 2-4. Three out of four Motive scores are on the way up while this couple enjoys a hot tub soak.

Hunger, Bladder, Energy, and Comfort are the most demanding of Motives, because if any one score drops below a certain level, the Sim will immediately exit his or her current activity to remedy the deficit. The following table lists the exit triggers for each category.

Mandatory Exit Factors

MOTIVE	SIM TYPE	EXITS CURRENT INTERACTION WHEN MOTIVE DROPS BELOW
Bladder	Resident	-85
Bladder	Visitor	-80
Comfort	Resident	-90
Comfort	Visitor	-60
Energy	Resident	-80
Energy	Visitor	-70
Hunger	Resident	-80
Hunger	Visitor	-40

Hygiene

Bad Hygiene will never kill a Sim, although it may seriously gross out others in the immediate vicinity. Solving this problem is easy—have your Sims wash their hands or take a shower. You can also combine Hygiene with other Motives. Taking a bath boosts the Hygiene and Comfort scores, while a soak in the hot tub (with friends) rewards the Hygiene, Comfort, Social, and Fun Motive bars.

Bladder

If you can't satisfy the Bladder urge, you'll be cleaning up puddles on the floor. Just make sure you find a bathroom before the Motive bar turns full red. A Sloppy Sim creates an additional risk by not regularly flushing the toilet. If you don't issue timely reminders, the toilet could get clogged, causing a major mess.

TIP

Pay special attention to the Bladder bar when your Sim spends time at the Beverage Bar or drinks a lot of coffee.

CAUTION

The Hygiene score takes a nose dive if a Sim can't get to the bathroom in time and pees on the floor.

Fig. 2-5. This Sim's Bladder is not quite full, but unless his guest vacates the bathroom soon, he could be in trouble.

Energy

We're talking sleep, pure and simple. Ideally, a good night's sleep should turn the bar completely green. This will happen at varying rates, depending upon the quality of the mattress, so you can get by on less sleep if you splurge for an expensive bed. If your Sim can't get to the bedroom or a couch before the Energy bar turns completely red, the floor becomes your only option. If this happens, wake your Sim and find the closest bed. A night on the hard floor will degrade your Sim's Comfort level to zero, while only restoring partial energy.

If your Sim stays up too late playing computer games, a shot of espresso provides a temporary Energy boost, although it will also fill the Bladder at an increased rate. Espresso has a powerful effect, but it takes longer to consume, which could be a problem if the car pool driver is honking.

Fig. 2-6. It never hurts to send your kids to bed early, because if they are tired in the morning, a coffee jolt is not an option.

Fun

Sims like to cut loose from the daily grind and have Fun, but depending upon their personalities, they prefer different activities. For example, a Playful Sim leans toward computer games, pinball machines, and train sets; while a more Serious Sim would rather sit down to a quiet game of chess or spend a few minutes gazing at a painting.

Fig. 2-7. These two Sims enjoy a game of pool after work.

Kids need to have more Fun than adults, and the effects of a single play session deteriorate faster for kids than for their older counterparts. Hence, it is a good idea to fill the house with plenty of juvenile diversions if you have children.

There are four different types of Fun activities: Extended, One-Time, Timed, and Endless. The following lists and tables provide additional information, including exit factors, for these pursuits.

Extended Fun Activities

Sims exit the following extended activities after reaching the maximum Fun score for their personality types. Hence, a Playful, Active Sim will stay on the basketball court longer than a Serious Sim.

- Basketball Hoop
- Bookshelf (reading)
- Dollhouse
- Computer (playing games)
- Pinball Machine
- Play Structure
- Stereo
- Toy Box
- Train Set
- TV
- VR Glasses

One-Time Fun Activities

The following activities raise a Sim's Fun score once with each interaction. It may take several interactions with the same activity for a Sim to reach the maximum Fun level.

OBJECT	ACTION
Aquarium	Feed or watch fish
Baby	Play
Diving Board	Dive into the pool
Espresso Machine	Drink espresso
Fountain	View
Lava Lamp	View
Painting	View
Sculpture	View

Timed (Pre-set) Fun Activities

As with the one-time activities listed above, a Sim may need to repeat the following activities to achieve maximum Fun points.

- Chess Set
- Pool Table

Endless Fun

- **Hot Tub:** A Sim will stay in the tub until Fun, Comfort, Social, and Hygiene numbers reach maximum levels.
- **Swimming Pool:** A Sim will keep doing laps until another Motive takes effect, or until you assign him or her to another activity.

Social

Sims crave other Sims, especially if they are Outgoing. Although they won't die without socializing, it is a good idea to devote a portion of each day to a group activity, even if it is a simple hot tub session with your Sim's mate, or a family meal.

Fig. 2-8. A casual conversation during breakfast raises this Sim's Social score.

The following table summarizes all of the possible Social interactions between adults and children. We take this one step further in the next chapter, "Interacting with Other Sims," where we examine Relationships.

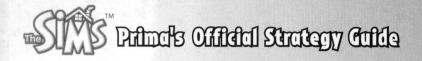
Adult-Child Interactions

ACTION	ADULT TO ADULT	CHILD TO CHILD	ADULT TO CHILD	CHILD TO ADULT
Apologize	X	—	—	—
Attack	X	X	—	—
Brag	X	X	X	X
Call Here	X	X	X	X
Cheer Up	X	X	X	X
Compliment	X	—	—	—
Dance	X	—	—	—
Entertain	X	X	X	X
Flirt	X	—	—	—
Give Back Rub	X	—	—	—
Give Gift	X	X	X	X
Hug	X	X	X	X
Insult	X	X	X	X
Joke	X	X	X	X
Kiss	X	—	—	—
Say Goodbye	X	X	X	—
Scare	X	X	X	X
Slap	X	—	—	—
Tag	—	X	—	—
Talk	X	X	X	X
Tease	X	X	X	X
Tickle	X	X	X	X

Social Outcome Modifiers

You didn't expect a Sim Social encounter to be simple, did you? When one Sim communicates with another, several calculations determine the outcome. Factors include age (adult or child), sex, mood, and personality traits, not to mention the current state of their Relationship. Also, a Sim with strong Social needs (but few friends) may expect more from an encounter with a Sim who has similar needs.

The following table lists the factors that govern the choices that appear on a Social actions menu. For example, two Sims who are strangers are not likely to have the options to kiss or hug. Additionally, the table lists key factors that determine the eventual outcome.

rel = Relationship

out = Outgoing

play = Playful

ff = Friend Flag

ss = Same Sex

rom = Romance Flag

age = Adult/Child

social = Social Motive Value

vis = Visitor

budget = Household Budget

nice = Nice

body = Body

Social Outcome Factors

INTERACTION	FACTORS THAT DETERMINE APPEARANCE ON THE MENU	FACTORS THAT DETERMINE OUTCOME
Apologize	rel	mood
Attack	age, nice, mood, rel	body
Back Rub	age, nice, mood, rel, out, ss	rel, out, ss
Brag	nice, out, social, rel	rel, mood
Cheer Up	ff, mood (of friend), nice	rel
Compliment	age, nice, out, mood, rel	rel, mood
Dance	age, mood, out, rel	rel, out, mood
Entertain	social, out, play, mood, rel	play, rel
Flirt	age, social, ss, out, mood, rel, rom	rel, mood, ss
Gift	vis, budget, nice, mood, rel	rel, mood
Hug	age, out, mood, rel, ss	rel, out, mood, ss
Insult	nice, mood, rel	nice
Joke	play, mood, rel	play, mood, rel
Kiss	ss, mood, rel, age	rel, mood, ss
Scare	nice, mood, play, rel	play, mood
Slap	age, nice, mood, rel	nice, mood
Talk	mood, rel, out	topics match
Tease	nice, mood, rel	rel, mood
Tickle	social, out, play, active, mood, rel	rel, play

Room

This is a combined rating that analyzes the design and contents of the current room, and translates it into a Room score. Of all the Motives, Room is the least important. However, if you love your Sim, you'll want to create the best possible environment. The most important contributing factors to Room score are:

- **Light:** Sims hate dark rooms, so fill your house with sunlight (windows and paned doors), lamps, and wall lights.
- **Room Size:** Don't cramp your Sims into tiny rooms.
- **Corners:** As mentioned in the "Building a House" chapter, Sims love corners.
- **State of Repair:** Any items that are not functioning properly detract from the Room score (see following list).

Fig. 2-9. Who wouldn't love a kitchen like this? It's bright, roomy, nicely furnished, and packed with high-tech appliances.

Negative Impact on Room Score

- Trash
- Floods
- Dirty plates
- Meals with flies
- Full trash cans/compactors
- Dead plants
- Puddle or ash pile
- Dead fish in aquariums
- Dirty objects (shower, toilet, tub)

The following table lists the positive or negative value of every object in *The Sims*.

Room Score

OBJECT	STATE/TYPE	ROOM SCORE
Aquarium	Fish Alive	25
	Dirty	-25
	Dirty and/or Dead	-50
Ash	N/A	-10
Bar	N/A	20
Bed	Unmade (Any Bed)	-10
	Made Mission	30
	Made (Other than Mission)	10
Chair	Parisienne	25
	Empress	10
Clock (Grandfather)	N/A	50
Computer	Broken	-25
Counter	Barcelona	15
Desk	Redmond	15
Dresser	Antique Armoire	20
	Oak Armoire	10
Fire	N/A	-100

OBJECT	STATE/TYPE	ROOM SCORE
Fireplace	Library Edition (No Fire)	20
	Library Edition (Fire)	75
	Worcestershire (No Fire)	15
	Worcestershire (Fire)	60
	Bostonian (No Fire)	10
	Bostonian (Fire)	45
	Modesto (No Fire)	5
	Modesto (Fire)	30
Flamingo	N/A	10
Flood	N/A	-25
Flowers (Outdoor)	Healthy	20
	Dead	-20
Flowers/Plants (Indoor)	Healthy	10
	Wilted	0
	Dead	-10
Food	Snack (Spoiled)	-15
	Fruitcake (Empty Plate)	-5
	BBQ Group Meal (Spoiled)	-20
	BBQ Single Meal (Spoiled)	-15
	Empty Plate	-10
	Pizza Slice (Spoiled)	-10
	Pizza Box (Spoiled)	-25
	Candy (Spoiled)	-5
	Group Meal (Spoiled)	-20
	Meal (Spoiled)	-25
	Quick Meal (Spoiled)	-20
Fountain	N/A	25
Flowers (Gift)	Dead	-10
	Alive	20
Lamp	Not Broken	10
Lava Lamp	N/A	20
Newspaper	Old Newspapers	-20
Piano	N/A	30

OBJECT	STATE/TYPE	ROOM SCORE
Pinball Machine	Broken	-15
Shower	Broken	-15
Sofa (Deiter or Dolce)	N/A	20
Stereo	Strings	25
Table	Mesa	15
	Parisienne	25
Toilet	Clogged	-10
Train Set	Small	25
Trash Can (Inside)	Full	-20
Trash Compactor	Full	-25
Trash Pile	N/A	-20
TV	Soma	20
	Broken (Any TV)	-15

Object Advertising Values

Earlier in the chapter we mentioned that Sims receive Motive rewards when they select an activity. If you are in complete control of your Sims (Free Will is off), you determine their choices. However, with Free Will on, Sims constantly poll their surroundings to compare which objects are "advertising" the most attractive rewards. The following table includes a Motive profile of every object in *The Sims*.

Object Advertising Values

OBJECT TYPE	POSSIBLE INTERACTIONS	OBJECT VARIATIONS	ADVERTISED MOTIVE	ADVERTISED VALUE	PERSONALITY TRAIT MODIFIER	REDUCED EFFECTS (OVER DISTANCE)
Aquarium	Clean & Restock	N/A	Room	30	Neat	Medium
	Feed Fish	N/A	Room	10	Nice	High
		N/A	Fun	10	Playful	High
	Watch Fish	N/A	Fun	10	Playful	High
Ash	Sweep Up	N/A	Energy	23	N/A	Medium
		N/A	Room	50	Neat	Medium
Baby	Play	N/A	Fun	50	Playful	Medium
Bar	Have Drink	N/A	Room	30	N/A	Low
	Grill	Barbecue	Energy	-10	N/A	Low
			Hunger	40	Cooking	Low
Basketball Hoop	Join	N/A	Fun	30	Active	High
		N/A	Social	20	N/A	Medium
		N/A	Energy	-20	N/A	Medium
	Play	N/A	Fun	30	Active	High
		N/A	Energy	-20	N/A	High
Bed	Make Bed	All Beds	Room	25	Neat	High
	Sleep	Double Bed (Cheap Eazzzzze)	Energy	65	N/A	None
		Double Bed (Napoleon)	Energy	67	N/A	None
		Double Bed (Mission)	Energy	70	N/A	None
		Single Bed (Spartan)	Energy	60	N/A	None
		Single Bed (Tyke Nyte)	Energy	63	N/A	None
	Tuck in Kid	All Beds	Energy	160	Nice	None

OBJECT TYPE	POSSIBLE INTERACTIONS	OBJECT VARIATIONS	ADVERTISED MOTIVE	ADVERTISED VALUE	PERSONALITY TRAIT MODIFIER	REDUCED EFFECTS (OVER DISTANCE)
Bookcase	Read a Book	Bookcase (Pine)	Fun	10	Serious	High
		Bookcase (Amishim)	Fun	20	Serious	High
		Bookcase (Libri di Regina)	Fun	30	Serious	High
Chair (Living Room)	Sit	Wicker	Comfort	20	N/A	Medium
		Country Class	Comfort	20	N/A	Medium
		Citronel	Comfort	20	N/A	Medium
		Sarrbach	Comfort	20	N/A	Medium
Chair (Dining Room)	Sit	Werkbunnst	Comfort	25	N/A	Medium
		Teak	Comfort	25	N/A	Medium
		Empress	Comfort	25	N/A	Medium
		Parisienne	Comfort	25	N/A	Medium
Chair (Office/Deck)	Sit	Office Chair	Comfort	20	N/A	Medium
		Deck Chair	Comfort	20	N/A	Medium
Chair (Recliner)	Nap	Both Recliners	Energy	15	Lazy	High
		Both Recliners	Comfort	20	Lazy	Medium
	Sit	Both Recliners	Comfort	30	Lazy	Medium
Chess	Join	Chess Set	Fun	40	Outgoing	High
			Social	40	N/A	Medium
	Play		Fun	35	Serious	High
Clock (Grandfather)	Wind	N/A	Room	40	Neat	High
Coffee (Espresso Machine)	Drink Espresso	N/A	Energy	115	N/A	Medium
		N/A	Fun	10	N/A	High
		N/A	Bladder	-10	N/A	High
Coffeemaker	Drink Coffee	N/A	Bladder	-5	N/A	High
		N/A	Energy	115	N/A	Medium

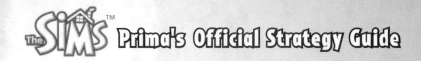

OBJECT TYPE	POSSIBLE INTERACTIONS	OBJECT VARIATIONS	ADVERTISED MOTIVE	ADVERTISED VALUE	PERSONALITY TRAIT MODIFIER	REDUCED EFFECTS (OVER DISTANCE)
Computer	Play	Moneywell	Fun	30	Playful	High
		Microscotch	Fun	35	Playful	High
		Brahma	Fun	40	Playful	High
		Marco	Fun	50	Playful	High
	Turn Off	All Computers	Energy	220	Neat	Medium
Dollhouse	Play	N/A	Fun	30	Playful	High
	Watch	N/A	Fun	30	Playful	Medium
		N/A	Social	30	N/A	Medium
Easel	Paint	N/A	Fun	20	N/A	High
Flamingo	Kick	N/A	Mood	15	Grouchy	High
	View	N/A	Fun	10	Playful	High
Flood	Clean	N/A	Room	80	Neat	High
Flowers (Outdoor)	Stomp On	N/A	Mood	10	Grouchy	High
	Water	N/A	Room	20	Neat	Medium
Flowers/Plants (Indoor)	Throw Out	N/A	Room	50	Neat	Medium
	Water	N/A	Room	25	Neat	Medium
Food	Clean	All Meal/ Snack Types	Room	20	Neat	Medium
	Prepare and Eat	BBQ Group Meal	Hunger	90	N/A	Low
		BBQ Single	Hunger	80	N/A	Low
		Candy	Hunger	30	N/A	Low
		Fruitcake (Group Meal)	Hunger	30	N/A	Low
		Fruitcake (Slice)	Hunger	80	N/A	Low
		Light Meal	Hunger	80	N/A	Low
		Pizza Box	Hunger	90	N/A	Low
		Pizza Slice	Hunger	80	N/A	Low
		Regular Group Meal	Hunger	90	N/A	Low
		Regular Single Meal	Hunger	80	N/A	Low
		Snack	Hunger	25	N/A	Low

OBJECT TYPE	POSSIBLE INTERACTIONS	OBJECT VARIATIONS	ADVERTISED MOTIVE	ADVERTISED VALUE	PERSONALITY TRAIT MODIFIER	REDUCED EFFECTS (OVER DISTANCE)
Fountain	Play	N/A	Fun	10	Shy	High
Refrigerator	Have Meal	All Fridges	Hunger	65	N/A	Low
	Have Snack	Llamark	Hunger	20	N/A	Low
		Porcina	Hunger	30	N/A	Low
		Freeze Secret	Hunger	40	N/A	Low
	Have Quick Meal	All Fridges	Hunger	55	N/A	Low
	Serve Meal	All Fridges	Hunger	70	Cooking	Low
		All Fridges	Energy	-10	N/A	Low
Gift (Flowers)	Clean	N/A	Room	30	Neat	Medium
Hot Tub	Get In	N/A	Fun	45	Lazy	High
		N/A	Comfort	50	N/A	High
		N/A	Social	25	Outgoing	Medium
		N/A	Hygiene	5	N/A	Medium
	Join	N/A	Comfort	30	N/A	Low
		N/A	Fun	50	Outgoing	Low
		N/A	Social	50	N/A	Low
		N/A	Hygiene	5	N/A	Medium
Lava Lamp	Turn On	N/A	Room	5	N/A	High
		N/A	Fun	5	N/A	High
Mailbox	Get Mail	N/A	Comfort	10	N/A	High
		N/A	Hunger	10	N/A	High
		N/A	Hygiene	10	N/A	High
		N/A	Room	10	N/A	High
Medicine Cabinet	Brush Teeth	N/A	Hygiene	25	Neat	Medium
Newspaper	Clean Up	N/A	Room	50	Neat	Medium
	Read	N/A	Fun	5	Serious	High
Painting	View	N/A	Fun	5	Serious	High
Phone	Answer	N/A	Fun	50	N/A	Medium
		N/A	Comfort	50	N/A	Medium
		N/A	Social	50	N/A	Medium
Piano	Play	N/A	Fun	40	Strong Creativity	High
	Watch	N/A	Fun	70	N/A	Medium
		N/A	Social	10	N/A	Medium

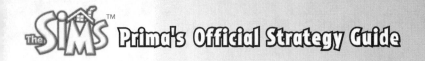

OBJECT TYPE	POSSIBLE INTERACTIONS	OBJECT VARIATIONS	ADVERTISED MOTIVE	ADVERTISED VALUE	PERSONALITY TRAIT MODIFIER	REDUCED EFFECTS (OVER DISTANCE)
Pinball Machine	Join	N/A	Fun	50	N/A	Medium
		N/A	Social	30	N/A	Medium
	Play	N/A	Fun	40	Playful	High
Play Structure	Join	N/A	Fun	60	Playful	Medium
		N/A	Social	40	N/A	Medium
	Play	N/A	Fun	60	Playful	Medium
Pool Diving Board	Dive In	N/A	Fun	35	Active	High
		N/A	Energy	-10	N/A	High
Pool Table	Join	N/A	Fun	50	Playful	Low
		N/A	Social	40	N/A	Low
	Play	N/A	Fun	45	Playful	High
Sculpture	View	Scylla and Charybdis	Fun	6	Serious	High
		Bust of Athena	Fun	5	Serious	High
		Large Black Slab	Fun	8	Serious	High
		China Vase	Fun	7	Serious	High
Shower	Clean	N/A	Room	20	Neat	High
	Take a Shower	N/A	Hygiene	50	Neat	Medium
Sink	Wash Hands	N/A	Hygiene	10	Neat	High
Sofa/Loveseat	Nap	All Sofas/ Loveseats	Energy	40	Lazy	High
		All Sofas/ Loveseats	Comfort	5	Lazy	High
	Sit	All Sofas/ Loveseats	Comfort	30	Lazy	Medium
		Garden Bench	Comfort	30	Lazy	Medium
Stereo	Dance	Boom Box	Social	40	Outgoing	High
			Fun	50	Active	High
		Zimantz Hi-Fi	Social	50	Outgoing	High
			Fun	60	Active	High
		Strings Theory	Social	60	Outgoing	High
			Fun	70	Active	High
	Join	Boom Box	Social	40	Outgoing	Low

OBJECT TYPE	POSSIBLE INTERACTIONS	OBJECT VARIATIONS	ADVERTISED MOTIVE	ADVERTISED VALUE	PERSONALITY TRAIT MODIFIER	REDUCED EFFECTS (OVER DISTANCE)
Stereo			Fun	40	Outgoing	Low
		Zimantz Hi-Fi	Social	50	Outgoing	Low
			Fun	40	Outgoing	Low
		Strings Theory	Social	60	Outgoing	Low
			Fun	40	Outgoing	Low
	Turn Off	All Stereos	Energy	220	Neat	Medium
	Turn On	Boom Box	Fun	25	Playful	High
		Zimantz Hi-Fi	Fun	25	Playful	High
		Strings Theory	Fun	30	Playful	High
Toilet	Clean	Both Toilets	Room	40	Neat	High
	Flush	Hygeia-O-Matic	Room	30	Neat	High
	Unclog	Both Toilets	Room	50	Neat	High
	Use	Hygeia-O-Matic	Bladder	50	N/A	Low
		Flush Force	Bladder	70	N/A	Low
Tombstone/ Urn	Mourn (first 24 hours)	N/A	Bladder	5	N/A	Low
		N/A	Comfort	50	N/A	Low
		N/A	Energy	5	N/A	Low
		N/A	Fun	50	N/A	Low
		N/A	Hunger	5	N/A	Low
		N/A	Hygiene	50	N/A	Low
		N/A	Social	50	N/A	Low
		N/A	Room	50	N/A	Low
	Mourn (second 48 hours)	N/A	Bladder	0	N/A	Low
		N/A	Comfort	30	N/A	Low
		N/A	Energy	0	N/A	Low
		N/A	Fun	30	N/A	Low
		N/A	Hunger	0	N/A	Low
		N/A	Hygiene	30	N/A	Low
		N/A	Social	30	N/A	Low
		N/A	Room	30	N/A	Low
Toy Box	Play	N/A	Fun	55	Playful	Medium

OBJECT TYPE	POSSIBLE INTERACTIONS	OBJECT VARIATIONS	ADVERTISED MOTIVE	ADVERTISED VALUE	PERSONALITY TRAIT MODIFIER	REDUCED EFFECTS (OVER DISTANCE)
Train Set (Large)	Play	N/A	Fun	40	N/A	Medium
	Watch	N/A	Fun	40	N/A	Low
		N/A	Social	40	N/A	Low
Train Set (Small)	Play	N/A	Fun	45	Playful	Medium
	Watch	N/A	Fun	20	N/A	Medium
		N/A	Social	30	N/A	Medium
Trash Can (Inside)	Empty Trash	N/A	Room	30	Neat	Medium
Trash Compactor	Empty Trash	N/A	Room	30	N/A	High
Trash Pile	Clean	N/A	Room	75	Neat	Medium
Bathtub	Clean	All Tubs	Room	20	Neat	High
	Bathe	Justa	Hygiene	50	Neat	Medium
		Justa	Comfort	20	N/A	Medium
		Sani-Queen	Hygiene	60	Neat	Medium
		Sani-Queen	Comfort	25	N/A	Medium
		Hydrothera	Hygiene	70	Neat	Medium
		Hydrothera	Comfort	30	N/A	Medium
TV	Join	Monochrome	Fun	20	Lazy	High
		Trottco	Fun	30	Lazy	High
		Soma Plasma	Fun	45	Lazy	High
	Turn Off	All TVs	Energy	220	Neat	Medium
	Turn On	Monochrome	Fun	18	Lazy	High
		Trottco	Fun	35	Lazy	High
		Soma Plasma	Fun	49	Lazy	High
	Watch TV	Monochrome	Fun	18	Lazy	High
		Trottco	Fun	28	Lazy	High
		Soma Plasma	Fun	42	Lazy	High
VR Glasses	Play	N/A	Fun	60	Playful	High

CHAPTER 3:
INTERACTING WITH
OTHER SIMS

Introduction

Once you get beyond the dark attraction of watching jilted Sims slap their rivals, or obnoxious Sims insulting their friends, you realize that Relationships are very important to your Sims' quality of life, and even to the advancement of their careers. In this chapter, we introduce you to the world of Relationships, covering the possible events that occur when two Sims come together verbally or physically. Our goal here is to lay down the ground rules. We'll offer hands-on tips for building and maintaining Relationships in the "All in the Family" chapter.

Relationship Scores

Icons representing a Sim's friendships, or lack thereof, appear in the screen's lower-right corner when you click on the Relationships icon (just above the Job icon). The scoring system ranges from below 0 (not good) to 100, which is reserved for one or more significant others. A relationship is considered a true friendship if the score climbs above 50. Only these Relationships are considered when the game calculates career advancements. Consult the next chapter, "9 to 5: Climbing the Career Ladder," for more information on promotion requirements.

Social Interactions

All Sim Relationships develop from Social interactions. If you don't spend quality time with your friends, the Relationships will deteriorate on their own, at a rate of two points per day. Of course, if you interact poorly, the rate accelerates dramatically. In the following sections, we review the myriad communication choices that are available during the game (grouped alphabetically by the active action). At any given time, your choice will vary, depending upon the level of your friendship, and whether or not your Sim is acting like a jerk!

Good Old Conversation

The easiest way to cultivate a new friendship is to talk. Sims communicate with each either using Sim-Speak, a delightful chatter that you actually begin to understand (yes, we have played this game way too much!). Adults and kids have favorite topics within their peer groups. These topics are randomly assigned by the game during the Sim creation process. Additionally, kids and adults have special cross-generational topics that are only used with each other. Active topics are displayed in thought balloons during the game, as shown in figure 3-2.

Fig. 3-1. This Sim Dad is clicking on all cylinders with his wife, but he needs to spend more time with the kids.

Fig. 3-2. Pets are a good common ground for conversation between adults and kids.

When a conversation is going well, you see a green plus sign over one or both of the Sims. Conversely, when talk deteriorates into the gutter, you'll see red minus signs. The following tables list positive and negative communications, including each potential outcome and the corresponding effect on Social and Relationship scores. For our purposes, an outcome is positive if it produces an increase in one or both scores. When scores drop or stay the same, it is considered a negative outcome.

Fig. 3-3. When two or more people enter a hot tub, the conversations begin spontaneously.

Positive Communications

INTERACTION	RESPONSE	RELATIONSHIP CHANGE	SOCIAL SCORE CHANGE
Apologize	Accept	10	15
Be Apologized To	Accept	10	15
Brag	Good	5	13
Be Bragged To	Good	5	7
Cheer Up	Good	5	7
Cheer Up	Neutral	0	5
Be Cheered Up	Good	10	10
Be Cheered Up	Neutral	0	5
Compliment	Accept	5	5
Be Complimented	Accept	5	11
Entertain	Laugh	4	7
Be Entertained	Laugh	8	13
Flirt	Good	5	13
Be Flirted With	Good	10	13
Joke	Laugh	5	13
Joke	Giggle	2	7
Listen to Joke	Laugh	7	13
Listen to Joke	Giggle	3	7
Scare	Laugh	5	10
TalkHigh Interest	Topic	3	5
TalkLike	Topic	3	5
Group Talk	N/A	1	8
Tease	Giggle	5	7

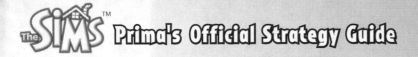

Negative Communications

INTERACTION	RESPONSE	RELATIONSHIP CHANGE	SOCIAL SCORE CHANGE
Apologize	Reject	-10	0
Be Apologized To	Reject	-10	0
Brag	Bad	-5	0
Be Bragged To	Bad	-5	0
Cheer Up	Bad	-3	0
Be Cheered Up	Bad	-10	0
Compliment	Reject	-10	0
Be Complimented	Reject	-7	0
Entertain	Boo	-15	0
Be Entertained	Boo	-7	0
Flirt	Refuse	-10	-17
Flirt	Ignore	-5	0
Be Flirted With	Refuse	-10	0
Be Flirted With	Ignore	0	0
Insult	Cry	5	0
Insult	Stoic	0	3
Insult	Angry	-10	7
Be Insulted	Cry	-12	-13
Be Insulted	Stoic	-5	-5
Be Insulted	Angry	-14	-7
Joke	Uninterested	-6	0
Listen to Joke	Uninterested	-7	0
Scare	Angry	-5	0
Be Scared	Angry	-10	0
TalkDislike	Topic	-3	3
TalkHate	Topic	-3	3
Tease	Cry	-4	0
Be Teased	Cry	-13	-7

Physical Contact

When a Relationship moves past the 50-point threshold, you begin to see new options on the Social interaction menu. Instead of just talking, you find new items including Hug, Give Back Rub, Flirt, and Kiss. It all depends upon how your Relationship is progressing and what the other Sim is looking for in the current interaction. The following tables include information on positive and negative physical events.

Positive Physical Events

INTERACTION	RESPONSE	RELATIONSHIP CHANGE	SOCIAL SCORE CHANGE
Give Back Rub	Good	5	7
Receive Back Rub	Good	9	13
Dance	Accept	8	13
Be Danced With	Accept	10	13
Give Gift	Accept	5	7
Receive Gift	Accept	10	13
Hug	Good	7	15
Hug	Tentative	2	7
Be Hugged	Good	8	15
Be Hugged	Tentative	4	7
Kiss	Passion	12	20
Kiss	Polite	5	10
Be Kissed	Passion	12	20
Be Kissed	Polite	5	10
Tickle	Accept	5	13
Be Tickled	Accept	8	13

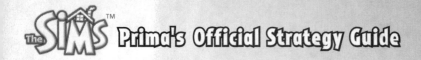

Negative Physical Events

INTERACTION	RESPONSE	RELATIONSHIP CHANGE	SOCIAL SCORE CHANGE
Attack	Win Fight	-5	10
Attack	Lose Fight	-10	-20
Give Back Rub	Bad	-7	0
Receive Back Rub	Bad	-10	0
Dance	Refuse	-5	0
Be Danced With	Refuse	-5	0
Give Gift	Stomp	-15	0
Receive Gift	Stomp	-5	0
Hug	Refuse	-10	0
Be Hugged	Refuse	-10	0
Kiss	Deny	-15	5
Be Kissed	Deny	-10	0
Slap	Cry	0	3
Slap	Slap Back	-10	-7
Be Slapped	Cry	-20	-17
Be Slapped	Slap Back	-15	7
Tickle	Refuse	-5	0
Be Tickled	Refuse	-8	0

CHAPTER 4:
9 TO 5—CLIMBING THE
CAREER LADDER

Introduction

When you first start playing *The Sims*, it's easy to get lost in the element. There's so much to explore and experience, and with more than enough money to furnish your house and buy a few toys, you can just hang out and live the good Sim-life. But, reality sets in sooner than you would like, and you must find a job. In this chapter we show you how to select a career, nurture the Skills necessary to earn the first few promotions, and finally, stockpile enough friends (it's called networking) to make the big bucks and zoom to the top of your field. For easy reference, we include comprehensive career tables that contain everything you need to know about the 10 Sim careers, including advancement requirements for all 10 pay levels.

Your First Job

Every Sim house receives a daily copy of the *Sim City Times* that includes a single job posting. You can take the first job you see, or buy a computer and view three jobs a day. There is no rush—you have enough money to get by for several days.

TIP

You can enjoy the free use of a computer by buying it, checking the want ads, and then returning it the same day for a full refund. Keep this up until you find the job you want. Then, later when you have more disposable cash, you can buy—and keep—a computer.

A Military job is usually available on the computer. This is an excellent first career, with a starting salary of §250. Furthermore, it remains the highest paying of the 10 careers through the first three advances. A Law Enforcement position is a close second.

Fig. 4-2. This two-commando family takes home §325 each as members of the Elite Forces (Level 2—Military Career).

If you would rather take your time and sort through all 10 job tracks, the following table will help you choose a career that is suited to your Sim's personality traits.

Fig. 4-1. Today's job posting is for a test driver.

Career Choices

CAREER TRACK	NECESSARY SKILLS	RELATED PERSONALITY TRAITS
Business	Logic, Charisma	Outgoing
Entertainment	Charisma, Creativity	Outgoing, Playful
Law Enforcement	Logic, Body	Active
Life of Crime	Creativity, Charisma	Playful, Outgoing
Medicine	Logic, Body	Active
Military	Repair, Body	Active
Politics	Charisma, Logic	Outgoing
Pro Athlete	Body, Charisma	Active, Outgoing
Science	Logic, Creativity	Playful
Xtreme	Creativity, Body/Charisma (tie)	Playful, Active, Outgoing

Developing Your Skills

After you decide on a career, focus on developing the appropriate Skills needed for advancement. It is important to remember that Sims do not study on their own. You need to direct your Sim to one of the activities listed in the Skill Enhancement table below.

On the control panel, click on the Job icon to display your Sim's current Skill bars (see figure 4-3). A white line designates the minimum level of Skill needed for the next promotion. Other factors contribute to earning a promotion, but without the Skill requirement, you have absolutely no chance for advancement to the next level.

Fig. 4-3. This Sim needs to boost his Body Skill one more notch, so he is scheduled for a session on the exercise machine right after lunch.

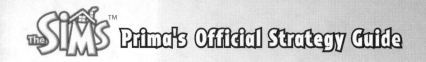

Skill Enhancement

SKILL	METHOD OF ENHANCEMENT	NOTES
Cooking	Bookshelf (Study Cooking)	Any type of bookshelf will suffice.
Mechanical	Bookshelf (Study Mechanical)	Any type of bookshelf will suffice.
Body	Exercise Machine (Work Out)	Exercise machine increases Skill four times faster than the pool. Active Sims improve their Skill at a higher rate.
	Pool (Swim)	See above.
Charisma	Mirrors or Medicine Cabinet (Practice Speech)	Outgoing Sims acquire Skill more quickly.
	Easel (Paint)	Playful Sims acquire Skill more quickly.
	Piano (Play)	Playful Sims acquire Skill more quickly.
Logic	Chessboard (Play)	Playing with another Sim generates Social points.

Fig. 4-4. A session on the exercise bench nets a Body point for this Sim.

Sim Career Tracks

The following tables include the salaries, hours, car pool vehicles, and job level requirements for each level of the 10 Sim career tracks. The Daily Motive Decay value shows which Motives deteriorate while the Sim is on the job.

Requirements for Level 1 Positions

CAREER TRACK	POSITION	PAY	HOURS	CAR POOL VEHICLE	COOKING	REPAIR	CHARISMA	BODY	LOGIC	CREATIVITY	FAMILY/ FRIENDS	DAILY MOTIVE DECAY						
												HUNGER	COMFORT	HYGIENE	BLADDER	ENERGY	FUN	SOCIAL
Business	Mail Room	§120	9 a.m.–3 p.m.	Junker	0	0	0	0	0	0	0	0	0	0	0	-30	0	0
Entertainment	Waiter Waitress	§100	9 a.m.–3 p.m.	Junker	0	0	0	0	0	0	0	0	0	0	0	-30	0	0
Law Enforcement	Security Guard	§240	12 a.m.–6 a.m.	Squad Car	0	0	0	0	0	0	0	0	0	0	0	-30	0	0
Life of Crime	Pickpocket	§140	9 a.m.–3 p.m.	Junker	0	0	0	0	0	0	0	0	0	0	0	-30	0	0
Medicine	Medical Technician	§200	9 a.m.–3 p.m.	Junker	0	0	0	0	0	0	0	0	0	0	0	-30	0	0
Military	Recruit	§250	6 a.m.–12 p.m.	Military Jeep	0	0	0	0	0	0	0	0	0	-15	0	-30	0	0
Politics	Campaign Work	§220	9 a.m.–6 p.m.	Junker	0	0	0	0	0	0	0	0	0	0	0	-30	0	0
Pro Athlete	Team Mascot	§110	12 p.m.–6 p.m.	Junker	0	0	0	0	0	0	0	0	0	-5	0	-35	0	0
Science	Test Subject	§155	9 a.m.–3 p.m.	Junker	0	0	0	0	0	0	0	0	0	0	0	-30	0	0
Extreme	Daredevil	§175	9 a.m.–3 p.m.	Junker	0	0	0	0	0	0	0	0	0	0	0	-30	0	0

Requirements for Level 2 Positions

CAREER TRACK	POSITION	PAY	HOURS	CAR POOL VEHICLE	COOKING	REPAIR	CHARISMA	BODY	LOGIC	CREATIVITY	FAMILY/ FRIENDS	DAILY MOTIVE DECAY						
												HUNGER	COMFORT	HYGIENE	BLADDER	ENERGY	FUN	SOCIAL
Business	Executive Assistant	§180	9 a.m.–4 p.m	Junker	0	0	0	0	0	0	0	0	0	0	0	-34	-2	0
Entertainment	Extra	§150	9 a.m.–3 p.m.	Junker	0	0	0	0	0	0	0	0	0	0	0	-34	-2	0
Law Enforcement	Cadet	§320	9 a.m.–3 p.m.	Squad Car	0	0	0	0	0	0	0	0	0	0	0	-34	-2	0
Life of Crime	Bagman	§200	11 p.m.–7 a.m.	Junker	0	0	0	0	0	0	0	0	0	0	0	-34	-2	0
Medicine	Paramedic	§275	11 p.m.–5 a.m.	Junker	0	0	0	0	0	0	0	0	0	0	0	-34	-2	0
Military	Elite Forces	§325	7 a.m.–1 p.m.	Military Jeep	0	0	0	0	0	0	0	0	0	-15	0	-34	-2	0
Politics	Intern	§300	9 a.m.–3 p.m.	Junker	0	0	0	0	0	0	0	0	0	0	0	-34	-2	0
Pro Athlete	Minor Leaguer	§170	9 a.m.–3 p.m.	Junker	0	0	0	0	0	0	0	0	0	-10	0	-40	-2	0
Science	Lab Assistant	§230	11 p.m.–5 a.m.	Junker	0	0	0	0	0	0	0	0	0	0	0	-34	-2	0
Extreme	Bungee Jump Instructor	§250	9 a.m.–3 p.m.	Junker	0	0	0	0	0	0	0	0	0	0	0	-34	-2	0

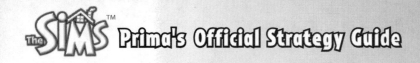

Requirements for Level 3 Positions

Career Track	Position	Pay	Hours	Car Pool Vehicle	Cooking	Repair	Charisma	Body	Logic	Creativity	Family/ Friends	Daily Motive Decay						
												Hunger	Comfort	Hygiene	Bladder	Energy	Fun	Social
Business	Field Sales Rep	§250	9 a.m.–4 p.m.	Junker	0	2	0	0	0	0	0	-3	0	-5	0	-38	-4	0
Entertainment	Bit Player	§200	9 a.m.–3 p.m.	Junker	0	0	2	0	0	0	0	-3	0	-5	0	-38	-4	0
Law Enforcement	Patrol Officer	§380	5 p.m.–1 a.m.	Squad Car	0	0	0	2	0	0	0	-3	0	-5	0	-38	-4	0
Life of Crime	Bookie	§275	12 p.m.–7 p.m.	Standard Car	0	0	0	2	0	0	0	-3	0	-5	0	-38	-4	0
Medicine	Nurse	§340	9 a.m.–3 p.m.	Standard Car	0	2	0	0	0	0	0	-3	0	-5	0	-38	-4	0
Military	Drill Instructor	§250	8 a.m.–2 p.m.	Military Jeep	0	0	0	2	0	0	0	-3	0	-20	0	-38	-4	0
Politics	Lobbyist	§360	9 a.m.–3 p.m.	Standard Car	0	0	2	0	0	0	0	-3	0	-5	0	-38	-4	0
Pro Athlete	Rookie	§230	9 a.m.–3 p.m.	Junker	0	0	0	2	0	0	0	-3	0	-15	0	-45	-2	0
Science	Field Researcher	§320	9 a.m.–3 p.m.	Standard Car	0	0	0	0	2	0	0	-3	0	-5	0	-38	-4	0
Xtreme	Whitewater Guide	§325	9 a.m.–3 p.m.	SUV	0	0	0	2	0	0	1	-3	0	-10	0	-45	-4	0

Requirements for Level 4 Positions

Career Track	Position	Pay	Hours	Car Pool Vehicle	Cooking	Repair	Charisma	Body	Logic	Creativity	Family/ Friends	Daily Motive Decay						
												Hunger	Comfort	Hygiene	Bladder	Energy	Fun	Social
Business	Junior Executive	§320	9 a.m.–4 p.m.	Standard Car	0	2	2	0	0	0	1	-7	0	-10	0	-42	-7	0
Entertainment	Stunt Double	§275	9 a.m.–4 p.m.	Standard Car	0	0	2	2	0	0	2	-7	0	-10	0	-42	-7	0
Law Enforcement	Desk Sergeant	§440	9 a.m.–3 p.m.	Squad Car	0	2	0	2	0	0	1	-7	0	-10	0	-42	-7	0
Life of Crime	Con Artist	§350	9 a.m.–3 p.m.	Standard Car	0	0	1	2	0	1	2	-7	0	-10	0	-42	-7	0
Medicine	Intern	§410	9 a.m.–6 p.m.	Standard Car	0	2	0	2	0	0	2	-7	0	-10	0	-42	-7	0
Military	Junior Officer	§450	9 a.m.–3 p.m.	Military Jeep	0	1	2	2	0	0	0	-7	0	-20	0	-42	-8	0
Politics	Campaign Manager	§430	9 a.m.–6 p.m.	Standard Car	0	0	2	0	1	0	2	-7	0	-10	0	-42	-7	0
Pro Athlete	Starter	§300	9 a.m.–3 p.m.	Standard Car	0	0	0	5	0	0	1	-7	0	-20	0	-50	-2	0
Science	Science Teacher	§375	9 a.m.–4 p.m.	Standard Car	0	0	1	0	3	0	1	-7	0	-10	0	-40	-7	0
Xtreme	Xtreme Circuit Pro	§400	9 a.m.–3 p.m.	SUV	0	1	0	4	0	0	2	-7	0	-20	0	-50	-2	0

Requirements for Level 5 Positions

CAREER TRACK	POSITION	PAY	HOURS	CAR POOL VEHICLE	COOKING	REPAIR	CHARISMA	BODY	LOGIC	CREATIVITY	FAMILY/ FRIENDS	DAILY MOTIVE DECAY						
												HUNGER	COMFORT	HYGIENE	BLADDER	ENERGY	FUN	SOCIAL
Business	Executive	§400	9 a.m. –4 p.m.	Standard Car	0	2	2	0	2	0	3	-10	0	-15	0	-46	-10	0
Entertainment	B-Movie Star	§375	10 a.m. –5 p.m.	Standard Car	0	0	3	3	0	1	4	-10	0	-15	0	-46	-10	0
Law Enforcement	Vice Squad	§490	10 p.m. –4 a.m.	Squad Car	0	3	0	4	0	0	2	-10	0	-15	0	-46	-10	0
Life of Crime	Getaway Driver	§425	5 p.m. –1 a.m.	Standard Car	0	2	1	2	0	2	3	-10	0	-10	0	-46	-10	0
Medicine	Resident	§480	9 p.m. –4 a.m.	Standard Car	0	3	0	2	2	0	3	-10	0	-15	0	-46	-10	0
Military	Counter-Intelligence	§500	9 a.m. –3 p.m.	Military Jeep	1	1	2	4	0	0	0	-10	0	-25	0	-46	-12	0
Politics	City Council Member	§485	9 a.m. –3 p.m.	Town Car	0	0	3	1	1	0	4	-10	0	-15	0	-46	-8	0
Pro Athlete	All-Star	§385	9 a.m. –3 p.m.	SUV	0	1	1	6	0	0	3	-10	0	-25	0	-55	-3	0
Science	Project Leader	§450	9 a.m. –5 p.m.	Standard Car	0	0	2	0	4	1	3	-10	0	-12	0	-43	-8	0
Xtreme	Bush Pilot	§475	9 a.m. –3 p.m.	SUV	1	2	0	4	1	0	3	-10	0	-15	0	-46	-5	-10

Requirements for Level 6 Positions

CAREER TRACK	POSITION	PAY	HOURS	CAR POOL VEHICLE	COOKING	REPAIR	CHARISMA	BODY	LOGIC	CREATIVITY	FAMILY/ FRIENDS	DAILY MOTIVE DECAY						
												HUNGER	COMFORT	HYGIENE	BLADDER	ENERGY	FUN	SOCIAL
Business	Senior Manager	§520	9 a.m. –4 p.m.	Standard Car	0	2	3	0	3	2	6	-14	0	-20	0	-50	-13	0
Entertainment	Supporting Player	§500	10 a.m. –6 p.m.	Limo	0	1	4	4	0	2	6	-14	0	-20	0	-50	-13	0
Law Enforcement	Detective	§540	9 a.m. –3 p.m.	Squad Car	1	3	1	5	1	0	4	-14	0	-20	0	-50	-13	0
Life of Crime	Bank Robber	§530	3 p.m. –11 p.m.	Town Car	0	3	2	3	1	2	4	-14	0	-15	0	-50	-13	-5
Medicine	GP	§550	10 a.m. –6 p.m.	Town Car	0	3	1	3	4	0	4	-14	0	-20	0	-50	-13	0
Military	Flight Officer	§550	9 a.m. –3 p.m.	Military Jeep	1	2	4	4	1	0	1	-14	0	-28	0	-50	-15	0
Politics	State Assembly-person	§540	9 a.m. –4 p.m.	Town Car	0	0	4	2	1	1	6	-14	0	-20	0	-50	-12	-3
Pro Athlete	MVP	§510	9 a.m. –3 p.m.	SUV	0	2	2	7	0	0	5	-14	0	-30	0	-60	-4	0
Science	Inventor	§540	10 a.m. –7 p.m.	Town Car	0	2	2	0	4	3	4	-14	0	-15	0	-45	-9	-8
Xtreme	Mountain Climber	§550	9 a.m. –3 p.m.	SUV	1	4	0	6	1	0	4	-14	0	-30	0	-60	0	0

Requirements for Level 7 Positions

CAREER TRACK	POSITION	PAY	HOURS	CAR POOL VEHICLE	COOKING	REPAIR	CHARISMA	BODY	LOGIC	CREATIVITY	FAMILY/ FRIENDS	DAILY MOTIVE DECAY						
												HUNGER	COMFORT	HYGIENE	BLADDER	ENERGY	FUN	SOCIAL
Business	Vice President	§660	9 a.m. –5 p.m.	Town Car	0	2	4	2	4	2	8	-18	0	-25	0	-54	-16	0
Entertainment	TV Star	§650	10 a.m. –6 p.m.	Limo	0	1	6	5	0	3	8	-18	0	-25	0	-54	-16	0
Law Enforcement	Lieutenant	§590	9 a.m. –3 p.m.	Limo	1	3	2	5	3	1	6	-18	0	-25	0	-54	-16	0
Life of Crime	Cat Burglar	§640	9 p.m. –3 a.m.	Town Car	1	3	2	5	2	3	6	-18	0	-20	0	-54	-16	0
Medicine	Specialist	§625	10 p.m. –4 a.m.	Town Car	0	4	2	4	4	1	5	-18	0	-25	0	-54	-16	0
Military	Senior Officer	§580	9 a.m. –3 p.m.	Military Jeep	1	3	4	5	3	0	3	-18	0	-31	0	-55	-20	0
Politics	Congress-person	§600	9 a.m. –3 p.m.	Town Car	0	0	4	3	3	2	9	-18	0	-25	0	-54	-18	-7
Pro Athlete	Superstar	§680	9 a.m. –4 p.m.	SUV	1	2	3	8	0	0	7	-18	0	-35	0	-65	-5	0
Science	Scholar	§640	10 a.m. –3 p.m.	Town Car	0	4	2	0	6	4	5	-18	0	-20	0	-48	-10	-10
Xtreme	Photo-journalist	§650	9 a.m. –3 p.m.	SUV	1	5	2	6	1	3	5	-18	0	-25	0	-54	-16	0

Requirements for Level 8 Positions

CAREER TRACK	POSITION	PAY	HOURS	CAR POOL VEHICLE	COOKING	REPAIR	CHARISMA	BODY	LOGIC	CREATIVITY	FAMILY/ FRIENDS	DAILY MOTIVE DECAY						
												HUNGER	COMFORT	HYGIENE	BLADDER	ENERGY	FUN	SOCIAL
Business	President	§800	9 a.m. –5 p.m.	Town Car	0	2	5	2	6	3	10	-22	0	-30	0	-58	-19	0
Entertainment	Feature Star	§900	5 p.m. –1 a.m.	Limo	0	2	7	6	0	4	10	-22	0	-30	0	-58	-19	0
Law Enforcement	SWAT Team Leader	§625	9 a.m. –3 p.m.	Limo	1	4	3	6	5	1	8	-22	0	-30	0	-58	-19	0
Life of Crime	Counterfeiter	§760	9 p.m. –3 a.m.	Town Car	1	5	2	5	3	5	8	-22	0	-25	0	-58	-19	-15
Medicine	Surgeon	§700	10 p.m. –4 a.m.	Town Car	0	4	3	5	6	2	7	-22	0	-30	0	-58	-19	0
Military	Commander	§600	9 a.m. –3 p.m.	Military Jeep	1	6	5	5	5	0	5	-22	0	-33	0	-60	-25	0
Politics	Judge	§650	9 a.m. –3 p.m.	Town Car	0	0	5	4	4	3	11	-22	0	-30	0	-58	-22	-11
Pro Athlete	Assistant Coach	§850	9 a.m. –2 p.m.	SUV	2	2	4	9	0	1	9	-22	0	-40	0	-70	-6	0
Science	Top Secret Researcher	§740	10 a.m. –3 p.m.	Town Car	1	6	4	0	7	4	7	-22	0	-25	0	-52	-12	-13
Xtreme	Treasure Hunter	§725	10 a.m. –5 p.m.	SUV	1	6	3	7	3	4	7	-22	0	-34	0	-60	-15	-5

Requirements for Level 9 Positions

CAREER TRACK	POSITION	PAY	HOURS	CAR POOL VEHICLE	COOKING	REPAIR	CHARISMA	BODY	LOGIC	CREATIVITY	FAMILY/ FRIENDS	HUNGER	COMFORT	HYGIENE	BLADDER	ENERGY	FUN	SOCIAL
												DAILY MOTIVE DECAY						
Business	CEO	§950	9 a.m. –4 p.m.	Limo	0	2	6	2	7	5	12	-26	0	-35	0	-62	-22	0
Entertainment	Broadway Star	§1100	10 a.m. –5 p.m.	Limo	0	2	8	7	0	7	12	-26	0	-35	0	-62	-22	0
Law Enforcement	Police Chief	§650	9 a.m. –5 p.m.	Limo	1	4	4	7	7	3	10	-26	0	-35	0	-62	-22	0
Life of Crime	Smuggler	§900	9 a.m. –3 p.m.	Town Car	1	5	5	6	3	6	10	-26	0	-30	0	-62	-22	-20
Medicine	Medical Researcher	§775	9 p.m. –4 a.m.	Limo	0	5	4	6	8	3	9	-26	0	-35	0	-62	-22	0
Military	Astronaut	§625	9 a.m. –3 p.m.	Limo	1	9	5	8	6	0	6	-26	0	-35	0	-65	-30	0
Politics	Senator	§700	9 a.m. –6 p.m.	Limo	0	0	6	5	6	4	14	-26	0	-35	0	-62	-26	-15
Pro Athlete	Coach	§1,000	9 a.m. –3 p.m.	SUV	3	2	6	10	0	2	11	-26	0	-45	0	-75	-8	0
Science	Theorist	§870	10 a.m. –2 p.m.	Town Car	1	7	4	0	9	7	8	-26	0	-30	0	-56	-16	-16
Xtreme	Grand Prix Driver	§825	10 a.m. –4 p.m.	Bentley	1	6	5	7	5	7	9	-26	0	-35	0	-62	-5	-10

Requirements for Level 10 Positions

CAREER TRACK	POSITION	PAY	HOURS	CAR POOL VEHICLE	COOKING	REPAIR	CHARISMA	BODY	LOGIC	CREATIVITY	FAMILY/ FRIENDS	HUNGER	COMFORT	HYGIENE	BLADDER	ENERGY	FUN	SOCIAL
												DAILY MOTIVE DECAY						
Business	Business Tycoon	§1,200	9 a.m. –3 p.m.	Limo	0	2	8	2	9	6	14	-30	0	-40	0	-66	-25	0
Entertainment	Super- star	§1,400	10 a.m. –3 p.m.	Limo	0	2	10	8	0	10	14	-30	0	-40	0	-66	-25	0
Law Enforcement	Captain Hero	§700	10 a.m. –4 p.m.	Limo	1	4	6	7	10	5	12	-20	-80	-45	-25	-60	0	0
Life of Crime	Criminal Mastermind	§1,100	6 p.m. –12 a.m.	Limo	2	5	7	6	4	8	12	-30	0	-35	0	-66	-25	-25
Medicine	Chief of Staff	§850	9 p.m. –4 a.m.	Hospital Limo	0	6	6	7	9	4	11	-30	0	-40	0	-66	-25	0
Military	General	§650	9 a.m. –3 p.m.	Staff Sedan	1	10	7	10	9	0	8	-30	0	-40	0	-70	-35	0
Politics	Mayor	§750	9 a.m. –3 p.m.	Limo	0	0	9	5	7	5	17	-30	0	-40	0	-66	-30	-20
Pro Athlete	Hall of Famer	§1,300	9 a.m. –3 p.m.	Limo	4	2	9	10	0	3	13	-30	0	-50	0	-80	-10	0
Science	Mad Scientist	§1,000	10 a.m. –2 p.m.	Limo	2	8	5	0	10	10	10	-30	0	-35	0	-60	-20	-20
Xtreme	International	§925	11 a.m. –5 p.m.	Bentley	2	6	8	8	6	9	11	-30	0	-30	0	-70	-20	-15

The Daily Grind

A working Sim needs to follow a schedule that is conducive to good job performance. Review the following tips as you devise a work schedule for your household.

Get Plenty of Sleep

Sims need to awake refreshed in order to arrive at work in a good mood. Send your Sims to bed early, and make sure there are no distractions (stereos, TVs, computers, etc.) that might interrupt their beauty sleep.

Fig. 4-5. Make sure your Sims get to bed early enough to restore maximum Energy before the alarm rings.

Set Your Alarm Clock

When set, the clock wakes your Sims two hours before the car pool arrives (one alarm clock takes care of the entire house). This is plenty of time to take care of Hunger, Bladder, and Hygiene Motive bars. If you still have time, improve your Sim's mood with a little non-strenuous fun like watching TV, or use the extra time to improve a Skill.

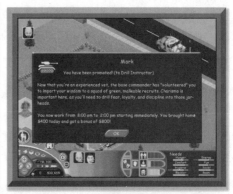

Fig. 4-6. That last set on the exercise bench paid off!

CAUTION

If two or more Sims in the house have jobs, the alarm clock rings for the earliest riser. Unfortunately, this wakes everyone else, regardless of when they have to be ready for the car pool. If you send the other Sims back to bed, you'll need to wake them manually, because the alarm clock only rings once each day.

Eat a Hearty Breakfast

When you're angling for a promotion, you need to arrive at work with all cylinders firing. When the alarm rings, send the designated house chef (the Sim with the highest Cooking Skill) to the kitchen to "Prepare a Meal." By the time your Sim is finished emptying his Bladder and completing necessary Hygiene, breakfast will be on the counter. There should be plenty of time to complete the meal and head to work with a full Hunger bar.

TIP

Make sure that your Sim is on the first floor and relatively close to the car pool within 15 minutes of departure to be sure he or she catches his or her ride. If you meet this deadline, your Sim will change clothes on the fly and sprint to the curb.

Make Friends and Influence Your Boss

Advancing through the first three levels does not carry a friendship requirement; however this ramps up very quickly. It helps to have a stay-at-home mate to concentrate on making friends. Remember that the career friendship requirement is for your household, not your Sim. So, if your mate or children have friends, they count toward your promotions, too.

Fig. 4-7. This Sim is just about out of Energy, but his Social score is maxed out and he's just made two new friends.

Take an Occasional Day Off to Recharge

If you find that your Sim is unable to have enough Fun or Social events to maintain a positive mood, skip a day of work and indulge. See a friend or two, work on Skills, or have some Fun. Just don't miss two days in a row or your Sim will be automatically fired!

Major Decisions

As you work your way up the career ladder, you encounter "major decisions" that involve various degrees of risk. They are winner-take-all, loser-gets-nada events that force you to gamble with your salary, integrity, or even your job. The following sections include a sample "major decision" for each career.

Business

Major decision: "Stock Option"

Player is given the choice of accepting a portfolio of company stock instead of salary for that pay period. The stock could double or tank. As a result, the player receives twice his salary or nothing at all for the pay period.

Entertainment

Major decision: "The Remake"

Your agent calls with an offer: Sim Studios wants you for the lead in a remake of *Citizen Kane*. Accepting will either send your Charisma sky high when the film succeeds wildly…or send it crashing if the turkey flops.

Law Enforcement

Major decision: "The Bribe"

A mobster you're investigating offers a huge bribe to drop the case. The charges won't stick without your testimony and you *could* suddenly "lose the evidence" and quietly pocket a nice nest egg…or get busted by Internal Affairs and have to start over on a new career track.

Life of Crime

Major decision: "The Perfect Crime"

You've just been handed a hot tip that an informant claims will be an easy knockover with loads of cash for the taking. Either the tip is gold, or it's a police sting. An arrest means your family is left at home alone while you're sent off to cool your heels in Sim City Prison for a while. If you succeed, your Charisma and Creativity Skills are enhanced.

Medicine

Major Decision: "Malpractice"

A former patient has slapped you with a massive malpractice suit. You can settle immediately by offering a payment equal to 50 percent of the cash in your household account. Or, take the bum to court. Lose, and all your furniture and household goods are repossessed. Win, and you receive a settlement equal to 100 percent of the cash in your household account.

Military

Major decision: "Gung Ho"

The general needs volunteers for a highly dangerous mission. You can refuse without penalty. If you accept, and succeed on the mission, you are decorated and immediately promoted to the next level. Failure means a demotion, soldier—you're broken down to the previous level.

Politics

Major decision: "Scandal"

An attractive young member of your team also happens to be heir to a fortune. He or she will finance your career advancement if you agree to "private consultations." You can refuse, with no change in status. Otherwise, there are two possible outcomes. You might get away with it and immediately advance *two* levels. If you're caught, you'll lose your friends when the scandal breaks in the media, and you'll be tossed from the career track to seek another.

Pro Athlete

Major Decision: "The Supermatch"

A one-on-one, pay-per-view contest pitting you against your greatest local rival is offered. If you win, it's worth double your paycheck. If you lose, the indignity comes complete with an injury costing you a reduction in your Body Skill along with a drop in Charisma. The player can always refuse at no penalty.

Science

Major decision: "The Experiment"

A science research firm is willing to pay you a fat bonus for conducting a complex experiment. However, the work must be conducted at your home, using rats as test subjects. Success means you collect the fee, with a bonus increase in your Logic Skill level. A failed experiment results in a dozen rats escaping into your home. That means a major bill from both your exterminator and your electrician (the rats have chewed through power cords.) Financial damage could be reduced if the Player's Repair Skills are strong.

Xtreme

Major decision: "Deep Freeze"

An arctic expedition is holding a spot open for you. It's a risky enterprise, so you may refuse. However, for a person in your particular line of work, that refusal will lower your Charisma. If you join the team, and they reach their goal, you will be rewarded with a considerable rise in Charisma. If the mission goes awry, your Sim is "lost on an iceberg" for a period of game time.

CHAPTER 5:
BUILDING A HOUSE

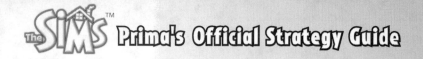

Introduction

Anyone who has ever built a home knows that the best laid plans of architects can sometimes turn into a house of horrors when the walls start going up. The same holds true in *The Sims*, where you have enough power to build a magnificent dream house or your worst residential nightmare. Limited only by your bank account, you can build a conservative dwelling that is functional above all else, or you can drop a family of eight in the middle of a meadow with only a bathroom and a refrigerator. It's all possible in *The Sims*, but rest assured that your family will deliver a quick—and sometimes scathing—critique when the clock starts ticking on their simulated lives.

In this chapter, we take you through the house design process from terrain preparation to landscaping. For demonstration purposes, we will use just about every building option available. Obviously, you would need a pile of Simoleans to do this in the game. However, we also cover important design considerations that enable you to maximize your Room score, regardless of your budget. In this chapter, we limit our discussion to the available options in Build Mode only. For detailed descriptions of more than 150 *Sims* objects, see the next chapter.

Of course, our suggestions are just the beginning. Sims thrive on the individuality of their creator, and if you want to build dungeons, sprawling compounds, or one-room huts, you have our support and encouragement. Remember, a bad house is no match for the bulldozer—your next house is only a click away!

Don't try to build your dream house at the beginning of the game. It's easier to tear down your original house and start over after you've fattened up your bank account.

Design Considerations

Before we introduce you to the various options available in Build Mode, here is a checklist for your basic floor plan. Invariably, your unique family of Sims will make their needs known to you as the game progresses. However, if you follow these house design basics, you should get your family off to a positive start with a minimum of emotional outbursts.

* **Don't worry about having room to expand. Build your first house to match the number of Sims in your family.**
* **Keep the bathroom centrally located. A door on either side allows quick access for emergencies.**
* **If you start with three Sims or more, build one or more half-bathrooms (toilet and sink only) to ease the crunch.**
* **Place the house close to the street, so you don't have to do the hundred yard dash to meet your car pool.**
* **Allow enough open wall for your kitchen countertops and appliances.**
* **Make your kitchen large enough to accommodate a small table and chairs.**
* **If you don't want a separate den or family room, make one of the bedrooms large enough to handle a computer desk and chair.**

Terrain Tools

In most locations, you can build a roomy house on a flat piece of land without having to level the terrain. However, if you want to build a house near the water or at the edge of a hill, you'll need to smooth the sloping tiles before building a wall, as displayed in figure 5-1.

Fig. 5-1. You can't place a wall section until you smooth the slope.

The Terrain Tool (shovel icon) can be a little tricky to master. On level ground, you can place the shovel at any intersection of horizontal and vertical grid lines, and then click to level, lower, or raise the tile. However, sometimes, due to extreme depth or elevation (usually at the edge of a gully or alongside water), you can't access this intersecting point. When this occurs, you receive a message telling you that the tile cannot be modified (figure 5-2).

The grid lines become noticeably darker when a previously elevated or lowered tile becomes level.

Fig. 5–2. You cannot level a tile at the water's edge.

In most cases, there is no need to edit the terrain, unless you want to add a sunken hot tub or drop an outdoor play set into a pit. Remember that you must level the ground in the pit before you can place an object (see figure 5-3).

Fig. 5-3. You cannot place the play set until the tiles in the pit are level.

Wall and Fence Tools

There are several tools here, but your first step is to "frame" your house. Simply place the cursor at any tile intersection. Then click, hold, and drag to place your wall (figure 5-4). When you release the mouse button, the wood framing will change to the type of wall you selected on the Control Panel (see page 52 for descriptions of wall types).

Fig. 5-4. Drag and release to place a wall.

TIP

Don't worry if you end up with a tree inside the walls of your house. You can build an atrium and keep the tree where it is, or use the Hand Tool to select the tree, and then move or delete it.

Although you must start a wall at an intersection, you are not limited to square walls. Simply drag the cursor at an angle to create an interesting corner (figure 5-5). However, don't make the angled walls too long. You cannot place doors, windows, or objects on these walls. Also, you cannot connect an angled wall to an existing straight wall inside your house.

TIP

To delete a wall, hold down the Ctrl key, then click and drag on a section of wall.

Wall Tool

Wall Types

NAME	COST (PER SECTION)	DESCRIPTION
White Picket Fence	§10	Outdoor fencing
Privacy Fence	§35	8-foot outdoor fence
Monticello Balustrade	§45	Railings for balconies and stairs
Wrought Iron Balustrade	§45	Railings for balconies and stairs
Tumbleweed Wooden Column	§70	Support columns for second stories or patio covers
Wall Tool	§70	Basic unfinished wall
The Zorba Ionic Column	§80	Classic, white Graeco-Roman column
Chester Brick Column	§100	All brick, squared off column

Fig. 5-5. Angled corners help you transform a boring box into a custom home.

TIP

Columns are not restricted to outside use. Try using the Zorba Ionic Column to create a beautiful entry from the living room into a formal dining room.

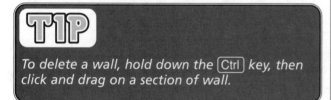

Door and Window Tools

Door Tool

Sims are very active. They seek the best path for their current task, and they think nothing of going out one exterior door and back in through another, if it's the best route. The least expensive Walnut Door (figure 5-6) is only §100, but because it is solid, your Room score does not benefit from outside light. If at all possible, invest in one of the windowed doors, and ideally, pick the multi-paned Monticello Door for maximum light.

Fig. 5-6. The Walnut Door gives your Sims privacy, but it doesn't allow outside light to improve your Room score.

Door Types

NAME	COST	NOTES
Walnut Door	§100	Solid door without windows
Maple Door Frame	§150	Wooden door frame for rooms that do not require total privacy
Federal Lattice Window Door	§200	Glass panes in the upper half of door
Windsor Door	§300	Designer leaded glass door
Monticello Door	§400	7 rows of 3 panes, topped with a 6-pane half circle, allow maximum light to flow into your home

Window Tool

Let the sun shine in to pump up your Room score. Sims love light, so install plenty of windows from the start. Simply click on the selected window and place it on any right-angle wall (remember, you cannot place doors, windows, or objects on a diagonal wall). Window style is strictly personal—all windows exert the same positive effect on the Room score.

 TIP

For aesthetic value, match your windows to your door style, such as the Monticello Door with Monticello Windows, as pictured in figure 5-7.

Fig. 5-7. Monticello Doors and Windows provide maximum light.

Window Types

NAME	COST	DESCRIPTION
Single-Pane Fixed Window	§50	This economy window still lets in the sun.
Single-Hung Window	§55	This looks good over the kitchen sink.
Privacy Window	§60	Tired of the neighborhood peeping Toms? This window is positioned higher on the wall.
Plate Glass Window	§65	This one's strictly glass from floor to ceiling.
El Sol Window	§80	This round ornamental window is a nice change from square and rectangular styles.
Monticello Window	§110	Use as a bedroom window to complement the Monticello door.
Windsor Window	§120	This ornamental natural wood window adds turn-of-the-century character to your home.
Monticello Window Full-Length	§200	This dramatic window looks beautiful on either side of a Monticello door.

Floor Tool

Unless you like grass in your living room, use the Floor Tool to lay some flooring inside your house. *The Sims* also includes outdoor flooring that works well in patios, backyard barbecue areas, or as pathways to a pool or play area. One tile covers a single grid, and you can quickly finish an entire room with a single shift-click. The price range for floor coverings is §10–§20, and you have a selection of 29 different styles/colors.

When you lay flooring inside a room with angled walls, half of the floor tiles appear on the other side of the wall, in another room or outside the house (see figure 5-8). To remove these outside tiles, place any floor type over the tiles, hold down the ⌈Ctrl⌉ key, and then click to delete them. The flooring on the other side of the wall remains undisturbed.

Fig. 5-8. After you finish the inside flooring, go back and delete the external tiles.

NOTE

You can use any type of flooring inside or outside.

Flooring Types

- **Carpeting (7)**
- **Cement (1)**
- **Ceramic Tile-Small Tiles (3)**
- **Checkerboard Linoleum (1)**
- **Clay Paver Tiles (1)**
- **Colored Pavement (1)**
- **Granite (2)**
- **Gravel (1)**
- **Hardwood Plank (1)**
- **Inlaid Hardwood (1)**
- **Italian Tile (1)**
- **Poured Concrete (1)**
- **Shale (1)**
- **Striped Pavement (2, Both Directions)**
- **Tatami Mats (2)**
- **Terracotta Tile (1)**
- **Wood Parquet (2)**

Wallpaper Tool

Fig. 5-9. Use the Wallpaper Tool to create a different mood in every room.

There are 30 different indoor/outdoor wall coverings in *The Sims,* and just as with floor coverings, you are limited only by your budget and sense of style. Prices range from §4 for basic wallpaper to §14 for granite block. If you change your mind after putting up the wallpaper, you can rip it down and get your money back by holding down the Ctrl key and clicking on the ugly panel.

Wallpaper Types

- **Adobe (1)**
- **Aluminum Siding (1)**
- **Brick (2)**
- **Granite (1)**
- **Interior Wall Treatments (6 Fabric and Paint Combinations)**
- **Japanese Paper/Screens (4)**
- **Paint (4)**
- **Plaster (1)**
- **Stucco (1)**
- **Tudor (1)**
- **Wainscoting (1)**
- **Wallpaper (4)**
- **Wood Clapboard (1)**
- **Wood Paneling (1)**
- **Wood Shingles (1)**

Stair Tool

You may not plan to build a second story immediately, but it's still a good idea to place your staircase before you start filling your house with objects. Choose from four staircases, two at §900 and two at §1,200. But, no matter how much you spend, they still get your Sims up and down the same way.

Style is considerably less important than function. You don't want to interrupt the traffic flow inside your house, especially to critical rooms such as the bathroom and kitchen. For this reason, staircases work well against a wall, where they are out of the way, or between two large, open rooms, such as the kitchen and family room (figure 5-10).

Fig. 5-10. Both of these placements keep the staircases out of the main traffic patterns.

If you don't have the money to finish the second story, just place the staircase and forget about it. The Sims won't go upstairs until you add a second story. After the staircase is positioned, the process for building a second story is exactly the same as building the first floor. The only obvious difference is that the buildable wall space extends out one square beyond the walls on the first floor. This allows you to squeeze a little extra space for a larger room or balcony.

Roof Tool

Although it is much easier to play *The Sims* using the Walls Cutaway or Walls Down options on the Control Panel, you will want to step back and enjoy your masterpiece in all of its crowning glory. The Roof Tool allows you to select a Shallow, Medium, or Steep Pitch for your roof, and choose from a selection of four roof patterns.

Fig. 5-11. Our house has a Steep Pitch with dark roof tiles.

Water Tools

Now that you have walls, floors, and doors, it's time to add a pool. Of course, this isn't a necessity, but your Sims love to swim, and it's an easy way to add important Body points. After placing your pool, don't forget to add a diving board so your Sims can get in, and a ladder so they can climb out. As you build your pool, the Water Tool places light-colored cement squares as decking. You can go back and cover these tiles with the outdoor surface of your choice, as displayed in figure 5-12. You can also add fencing around your deck to give your pool a more finished look.

Fig. 5-12. With the pool and decking in place, you have room to add an outdoor barbecue and beverage cart.

Fireplace Tool

Fig. 5-13. It looks innocent enough, but a roaring fire can turn nearby objects or Sims into a deadly inferno.

When placed safely out of the way of flammable objects, a fireplace adds a major boost to the Room score. However, it can be a dangerous fire hazard if Sims wander too close, so give it a wide berth when a fire is roaring.

Plant Tool

Now, it's time to put the finishing touches on the exterior of your house. Using the Plant Tool, you can select from 14 different plants, priced from §5 for Wildflowers to §300 for an Apple Tree. The following types of vegetation are included:

Plant Types

- **Flowers (4)**
- **Bushes (1)**
- **Hedges (2)**
- **Shrubs (2)**
- **Trees (5)**

Let your green thumb go wild, but don't forget that only trees and shrubs will thrive without regular watering. If you want colorful flowers, you'll probably need to hire a Gardener.

Fig. 5-14. This colorful landscaping will require the services of a Gardener, or a Sim with a lot of time to kill.

Special Editing Tools

In addition to the building tools described above, there are two other options on the Build Mode Control Panel. The curved arrows pictured at the bottom corner of figure 5-15 allow you to undo or repeat your last action(s). This is a quick way to delete unwanted items.

Fig. 5-15. Click Undo Last to reverse your most recent actions.

If the undo button is unavailable, you can click on the Hand Tool, select any object, and then press the Delete key to sell it back. For directions on how to delete walls, wall coverings, and floor coverings, see the appropriate sections in this chapter.

Fig. 5-16. Select an item with the Hand Tool, then press Delete to make it go away.

CHAPTER 6:
MATERIAL SIMS

Introduction

This chapter covers the eight categories of objects available in Buy Mode: Seating, Surfaces, Decorative, Electronics, Appliances, Plumbing, Lighting, and Miscellaneous. Every object is listed with its purchase price, related Motives, and Efficiency ratings. You can shop 'til you drop, but it's more important to buy smart than to buy often. Our comprehensive Buying Guide is just ahead, but first let's study some important factors that impact your spending habits.

Buying for Needs, Instead of Needing to Buy

If you select a ready-made house for your new Sim family, you acquire walls, floors, and a roof, but little else. The house is empty, with nary a toilet, bed, or refrigerator in sight. Depending upon how much you spent on the house, you'll have a few thousand Simoleans to use in Buy Mode, where you can purchase more than 150 objects. Most objects affect your Sims' environment in positive ways. However, not every object is a necessity. In fact, if you are a recovering shopping channel addict, this is not a good time to fall off your wallet. Make your first purchases with The Sims' Motives (or Needs) in mind. You can review your Sims' current Needs state by clicking on the Mood icon. We provide detailed descriptions in the Motives chapter, but for now, here is a basic shopping list that will help you get your Sims' Need bars out of the red zone during the early stages of a game.

TIP

In most instances, an expensive item has a greater impact on the related Need bar than an economy model. For example, a §300 cot gives your Sim a place to crash, but a §3,000 Mission Bed provides more Comfort and lets your Sim get by on less sleep. As an added bonus, the top-of-the-line bed also adds to the overall Room score.

Fig. 6-1. Despite logging only five hours of sleep, Bella is feeling pretty good, thanks to her §3000 Mission bed.

Fig. 6-2. A big-screen TV is fun for your Sims, but also for the neighbors, who will often hang out, and boost your Social score.

NEED	ITEM	EXPLANATION
Hunger	Refrigerator, Food Processor, Stove	A refrigerator alone will sustain life, but you will greatly improve the quality of Sim meals by using a food processor and stove. However, there is a risk of fire if your Sim doesn't have at least two Cooking Skill points.
Comfort	Bed, Chairs	Sims will sleep anywhere when they are tired, but a bed is highly recommended for sleeping, and you'll need chairs (for eating and working at the computer), and a couch for napping. A bathtub provides a little extra comfort for your Sims, but it isn't critical, provided you have a shower.
Hygiene	Sink, Shower	Dirty Sims spend a lot of time waving their arms in the air to disperse their body odor. Not a pretty sight. Fortunately, a sink and shower go a long way toward improving their state of mind (not to mention the smell).
Bladder	Toilet	When you gotta go, you gotta go. Sims prefer using a toilet, but if one is not available, they will relieve themselves on the floor. This not only causes great shame and embarrassment, but someone in your family will have to clean up the mess. It's also very bad for your Hygiene levels.
Energy	Bed	If you don't want to spawn a family of insomniacs, buy a sufficient number of beds for your Sims. A shot of coffee or espresso provides a temporary Energy boost, but it is definitely not a long-term solution.
Fun	TV	The boob tube is the easiest and cheapest way to give your Sims a break from their daily grinds. You can add other, more exciting, items later, but this is your best choice early on.
Social	Telephone	Ignore this for a short time while you focus on setting up your house. However, don't force your Sims into a solitary lifestyle. Other Sims may walk by the house, but you'll have better results after buying a telephone, so that you can invite people over and gain Social points when they arrive.
Room	Windows, Lamps, Decorations, Landscaping	Sims like plenty of light, from windows during the day and artificial lighting at night. Table Lamps are the cheapest, but they can only be placed on raised surfaces. As your game progresses, you can add decorations and landscaping to boost the Room score.

Sims Can Be Hard to Please

Given a fat bank account, it would seem that you can always cheer up your Sims with a few expensive purchases. Not exactly. While you are spending your hard-earned Simoleans, the Sims are busy comparing everything that you buy to everything they already own. If you fail to keep your Sims in the manner to which they are accustomed, their responses to your new objects may be indifferent or even downright negative. Every time you make a purchase, the game uses an assessment formula to calculate your Sim's response. The logic goes like this:

Fig. 6-3. Compared to the §2,100 "Snails With Icicles in Nose," this §45 clown picture doesn't quite stack up.

Your Diminishing Net Worth

When times are tough, you may need to raise cash by selling objects in your house. With rare exception, you will never match your initial investment, thanks to instant depreciation, and as time goes on, your belongings continue to lose value until they reach their depreciation limits. The following table lists every object in *The Sims* (alphabetically), including purchase price and depreciated values.

- Calculates the average value of everything in your house (including outdoor items).

- Subtracts 10 percent of the new object's value for each existing copy of the same item. Don't expect your family members to jump for joy if you add a hot tub to every room in the house.

- Compares the value of the new object with all existing objects in your house. If the new purchase is worth 20 percent or more above the average value of current items, the Sim exhibits a positive response by clapping.

- If the new object is within 20 percent (above or below) of the current average value of all items in your household, the Sim gives you an uninspired shrug.

- If the new object is less than 20 percent below the average value, your Sim waves it off and you'll see a red X through the object.

TIP

Although depreciation reduces the value of your furnishings over time, there is a buyer's remorse period when you can return the item for full value (if it has been less than 24 hours since you purchased it). So, if you have second thoughts about that new hot tub, simply select the item and hit the Delete key to get your money back.

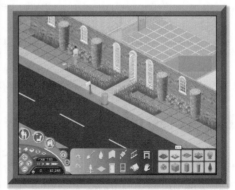

Fig. 6-4. This Pyrotorre Gas Range is §1,000 new, but after depreciation it's worth only §790.

Object Depreciation

NAME	PURCHASE PRICE	INITIAL DEPRECIATION	DAILY DEPRECIATION	DEPRECIATION LIMIT
Alarm: Burglar	§250	§62	§2	§50
Alarm: Smoke	§50	§12	§0	§10
Aquarium	§200	§30	§2	§80
Bar	§800	§120	§8	§320
Barbecue	§350	§70	§4	§105
Basketball Hoop (Cheap Eaze)	§650	§98	§6	§260
Bed: Double	§450	§68	§4	§180
Bed: Double (Mission)	§3,000	§450	§30	§1,200
Bed: Double (Napoleon)	§1,000	§150	§10	§400
Bed: Single (Spartan)	§300	§45	§3	§120
Bed: Single (Tyke Nyte)	§450	§68	§4	§180
Bench: Garden	§250	§38	§2	§100
Bookshelf: Amishim	§500	§75	§5	§200
Bookshelf: Libri di Regina	§900	§135	§9	§360
Bookshelf: Pine	§250	§38	§2	§100
Chair: Deck (Survivall)	§150	§22	§2	§60
Chair: Dining (Empress)	§600	§90	§6	§240
Chair: Dining (Parisienne)	§1,200	§180	§12	§480
Chair: Dining (Teak)	§200	§30	§2	§80
Chair: Dining (Werkbunnst)	§80	§12	§1	§32
Chair: Living Room (Citronel)	§450	§68	§4	§180
Chair: Living Room (Country Class)	§250	§38	§2	§100
Chair: Living Room (Sarrbach)	§500	§75	§5	§200
Chair: Living Room (Wicker)	§80	§12	§1	§32
Chair: Office	§100	§15	§1	§40

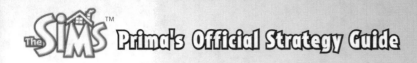

NAME	PURCHASE PRICE	INITIAL DEPRECIATION	DAILY DEPRECIATION	DEPRECIATION LIMIT
Chair: Recliner (Back Slack)	§250	§38	§2	§100
Chair: Recliner (Von Braun)	§850	§128	§8	§340
Chess Set	§500	§75	§5	§200
Clock: Alarm	§30	§4	§0	§12
Clock: Grandfather	§3,500	§525	§35	§1,400
Coffee: Espresso Machine	§450	§90	§4	§135
Coffeemaker	§85	§17	§1	§26
Computer (Brahma 2000)	§2,800	§700	§28	§560
Computer (Marco)	§6,500	§1,625	§65	§1,300
Computer (Microscotch)	§1,800	§450	§18	§360
Computer (Moneywell)	§999	§250	§10	§200
Counter: Bath (Count Blanc)	§400	§60	§4	§160
Counter: Kitchen (Barcelona: In)	§800	§120	§8	§320
Counter: Kitchen (Barcelona: Out)	§800	§120	§8	§320
Counter: Kitchen (NuMica)	§150	§22	§2	§60
Counter: Kitchen (Tiled)	§250	§38	§2	§100
Desk (Cupertino)	§220	§33	§2	§88
Desk (Mesquite)	§80	§12	§1	§32
Desk (Redmond)	§800	§120	§8	§320
Dishwasher (Dish Duster)	§550	§110	§6	§165
Dishwasher (Fuzzy Logic)	§950	§190	§10	§285
Dollhouse	§180	§27	§2	§72
Dresser (Antique Armoire)	§1,200	§180	§12	§480
Dresser (Kinderstuff)	§300	§45	§3	§120

NAME	PURCHASE PRICE	INITIAL DEPRECIATION	DAILY DEPRECIATION	DEPRECIATION LIMIT
Dresser (Oak Armoire)	§550	§82	§6	§220
Dresser (Pinegulcher)	§250	§38	§2	§100
Easel	§250	§38	§2	§100
Exercise Machine	§700	§105	§7	§280
Flamingo	§12	§2	§0	§5
Food Processor	§220	§44	§2	§66
Fountain	§700	§105	§7	§280
Fridge (Freeze Secret)	§2,500	§500	§25	§750
Fridge (Llamark)	§600	§120	§6	§180
Fridge (Porcina)	§1,200	§240	§12	§360
Hot Tub	§6,500	§1,300	§65	§1,950
Lamp: Floor (Halogen)	§50	§8	§0	§20
Lamp: Floor (Lumpen)	§100	§15	§1	§40
Lamp: Floor (Torchosteronne)	§350	§52	§4	§140
Lamp: Garden	§50	§7	§1	§20
Lamp: Love n' Haight Lava	§80	§12	§1	§32
Lamp: Table (Antique)	§300	§45	§3	§120
Lamp: Table (Bottle)	§25	§4	§0	§10
Lamp: Table (Ceramiche)	§85	§13	§1	§34
Lamp: Table (Elite)	§180	§27	§2	§72
Medicine Cabinet	§125	§19	§1	§50
Microwave	§250	§50	§2	§75
Mirror: Floor	§150	§22	§2	§60
Mirror: Wall	§100	§15	§1	§40
Phone: Tabletop	§50	§12	§0	§10
Phone: Wall	§75	§19	§1	§15
Piano	§3,500	§525	§35	§1,400
Pinball Machine	§1,800	§450	§18	§360
Plant: Big (Cactus)	§150	§22	§2	§60
Plant: Big (Jade)	§160	§24	§2	§64
Plant: Big (Rubber)	§120	§18	§1	§48

NAME	PURCHASE PRICE	INITIAL DEPRECIATION	DAILY DEPRECIATION	DEPRECIATION LIMIT
Plant: Small (Geranium)	§45	§7	§0	§18
Plant: Small (Spider)	§35	§5	§0	§14
Plant: Small (Violets)	§30	§4	§0	§12
Play Structure	§1,200	§180	§12	§480
Pool Table	§4,200	§630	§42	§1,680
Shower	§650	§130	§6	§195
Sink: Bathroom Pedestal	§400	§80	§4	§120
Sink: Kitchen (Double)	§500	§100	§5	§150
Sink: Kitchen (Single)	§250	§50	§2	§75
Sofa (Blue Pinstripe)	§400	§60	§4	§160
Sofa (Contempto)	§200	§30	§2	§80
Sofa (Country)	§450	§68	§4	§180
Sofa (Deiter)	§1,100	§165	§11	§440
Sofa (Dolce)	§1,450	§218	§14	§580
Sofa (Recycled)	§180	§27	§2	§72
Sofa (SimSafari)	§220	§33	§2	§88
Sofa: Loveseat (Blue Pinstripe)	§360	§54	§4	§144
Sofa: Loveseat (Contempto)	§150	§22	§2	§60
Sofa: Loveseat (Country)	§340	§51	§3	§136
Sofa: Loveseat (Indoor-Outdoor)	§160	§24	§2	§64
Sofa: Loveseat (Luxuriare)	§875	§131	§9	§350
Stereo (Strings)	§2,550	§638	§26	§510
Stereo (Zimantz)	§650	§162	§6	§130
Stereo: Boom Box	§100	§25	§1	§20
Stove (Dialectric)	§400	§80	§4	§120
Stove (Pyrotorre)	§1,000	§200	§10	§300
Table: Dining (Colonial)	§200	§30	§2	§80
Table: Dining (Mesa)	§450	§68	§4	§180

NAME	PURCHASE PRICE	INITIAL DEPRECIATION	DAILY DEPRECIATION	DEPRECIATION LIMIT
Table: Dining (NuMica)	§95	§14	§1	§38
Table: Dining (Parisienne)	§1,200	§180	§12	§480
Table: End (Anywhere)	§120	§18	§1	§48
Table: End (Imperious)	§135	§20	§1	§54
Table: End (KinderStuff)	§75	§11	§1	§30
Table: End (Mission)	§250	§38	§2	§100
Table: End (Pinegulcher)	§40	§6	§0	§16
Table: End (Sumpto)	§300	§45	§3	§120
Table: End (Wicker)	§55	§8	§1	§22
Table: Outdoor (Backwoods)	§200	§30	§2	§80
Toaster Oven	§100	§20	§1	§30
Toilet (Flush Force)	§1,200	§240	§12	§360
Toilet (Hygeia-O-Matic)	§300	§60	§3	§90
Tombstone/Urn	§5	§1	§0	§2
Toy Box	§50	§8	§0	§20
Train Set: Large	§955	§239	§10	§191
Train Set: Small	§80	§20	§1	§16
Trash Compactor	§375	§75	§4	§112
Tub (Hydrothera)	§3,200	§640	§32	§960
Tub (Justa)	§800	§160	§8	§240
Tub (Sani-Queen)	§1,500	§300	§15	§450
TV (Monochrome)	§85	§21	§1	§17
TV (Soma)	§3,500	§875	§35	§700
TV (Trottco)	§500	§125	§5	§100
VR Glasses	§2,300	§575	§23	§460

The Sims Buying Guide

The following sections represent the eight item categories that appear when you click the Buy Mode button on the control panel. We've added a few subcategories to make it easier to find a specific object. The Efficiency Value (1–10) indicates how well the item satisfies each Motive. You get what you pay for in *The Sims*, so an §80 chair doesn't quite stack up to an §850 recliner when it comes to boosting your Comfort level, and it cannot restore Energy.

Seating

Chairs

There are three types of chairs in *The Sims*: movable, stationary, and reclining. Any chair will function at a desk or table for eating and using objects. If your budget is tight, you can also use cheaper chairs for watching TV or reading, but their Comfort ratings are very low. You can use high-ticket dining room chairs at the computer, but that is probably overkill. You are better off placing them in the dining room where you receive greater benefit from their enhanced Room ratings.

Stationary chairs are cushier and nicely upholstered (depending on your taste, of course), and they usually provide more comfort. Finally, the reclining chairs are top of the line, giving you increased comfort and the added benefit of being able to catch a few Zs in the reclining position.

TIP

Chair placement is critical, especially around tables. A Sim will not move a chair sideways, only forward and backward. So, position the chair properly or the Sim will not be able to use the table (or what is on it). Also, be careful not to trap a Sim in a corner when a chair is pulled out. For example, if a child is playing with a train set in the corner of the room, and another Sim pulls out a chair to use the computer, the child would be trapped in the corner until the computer user is finished.

Werkbunnst All-Purpose Chair

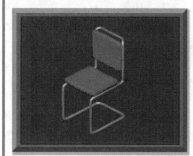

Type: Movable

Cost: §80

Motive: Comfort (2)

Posture Plus Office Chair

Type: Movable

Cost: §100

Motive: Comfort (3)

Deck Chair by Survivall

Type: Movable

Cost: §150

Motive: Comfort (3)

Parisienne Dining Chair

Type: Movable

Cost: §1,200

Motives: Comfort (6), Room (3)

Touch of Teak Dinette Chair

Type: Movable

Cost: §200

Motive: Comfort (3)

Sioux City Wicker Chair

Type: Stationary

Cost: §80

Motive: Comfort (2)

Empress Dining Room Chair

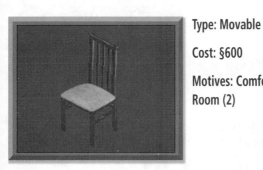

Type: Movable

Cost: §600

Motives: Comfort (4), Room (2)

Country Class Armchair

Type: Stationary

Cost: §250

Motive: Comfort (4)

"Citronel" from Chiclettina Inc.

Type: Stationary

Cost: §450

Motive: Comfort (6)

"The Sarrbach" by Werkbunnst

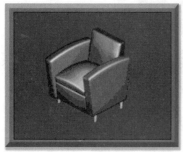

Type: Stationary

Cost: §500

Motive: Comfort (6)

"Back Slack" Recliner

Type: Recliner

Cost: §250

Motives: Comfort (6), Energy (3)

"Von Braun" Recliner

Type: Recliner

Cost: §850

Motives: Comfort (9), Energy (3)

Couches

Sitting down is fine for reading, eating, or working, but for serious vegging, your Sims need a good couch. When selecting a couch, function is more important than quality. If you are looking for a place to take naps, pay more attention to the Energy rating than the Comfort or Room ratings. A multipurpose couch should have good Energy and Comfort ratings. However, if you are furnishing your party area, select one that looks good, thereby enhancing your Room rating. Stay away from the cheapest couches (under §200). For a few extra dollars, a medium-priced couch will make your Sims a lot happier. When you're flush with Simoleans, don't forget to dress up your garden with the outdoor bench. You can't sleep on it, but it looks great.

Contempto Loveseat

Cost: §150

Motives: Comfort (3), Energy (4)

Indoor-Outdoor Loveseat

Cost: §160

Motives: Comfort (3), Energy (4)

SimSafari Sofa

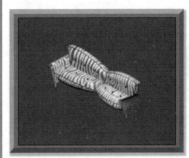

Cost: §220

Motives: Comfort (3), Energy (5)

Recycled Couch

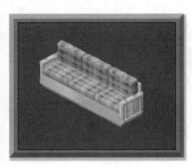

Cost: §180

Motives: Comfort (2), Energy (5)

Parque Fresco del Aire Bench

Cost: §250

Motive: Comfort (2)

Contempto Couch

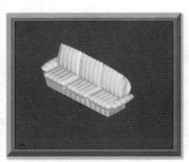

Cost: §200

Motives: Comfort (3), Energy (5)

Country Class Loveseat

Cost: §340

Motives: Comfort (5), Energy (4)

Pinstripe Loveseat from Zecutime

Cost: §360

Motives: Comfort (5), Energy (4)

Luxuriare Loveseat

Cost: §875

Motives: Comfort (8), Energy (4), Room (2)

Pinstripe Sofa from Zecutime

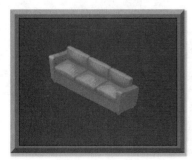

Cost: §400

Motives: Comfort (5), Energy (5)

"The Deiter" by Werkbunnst

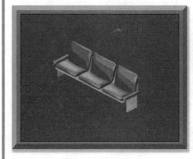

Cost: §1,100

Motives: Comfort (8), Energy (5), Room (3)

Country Class Sofa

Cost: §450

Motives: Comfort (5), Energy (5)

Dolce Tutti Frutti Sofa

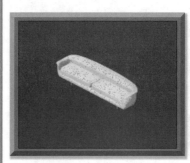

Cost: §1,450

Motives: Comfort (9), Energy (5), Room (3)

Beds

Getting enough sleep can be one of the most frustrating goals in *The Sims*, especially if there is a new baby in the house, or your car pool arrives at some ungodly hour of the morning. In the early stages of a game, it is not important to spend a bundle of money on a designer bed. However, an upgrade later on is well worth the money, because a top-of-the-line bed recharges your Energy bar faster.

Tyke Nyte Bed

Cost: §450

Motives: Comfort (7), Energy (7)

Spartan Special

Cost: §300

Motives: Comfort (6), Energy (7)

Napoleon Sleigh Bed

Cost: §1,000

Motives: Comfort (8), Energy (9)

Cheap Eazzzzze Double Sleeper

Cost: §450

Motives: Comfort (7), Energy (8)

Modern Mission Bed

Cost: §3,000

Motives: Comfort (9), Energy (10), Room (3)

Surfaces

Sims will eat or read standing up if they have to, but they won't be particularly happy about it. Sitting at a table while eating a meal bolsters a Sim's Comfort. Since your Sims have to eat to satisfy Hunger, they might as well improve Comfort, too. Many objects require elevated surfaces, so allow enough room for nightstands (alarm clock, lamps), tables (computer), and countertops (microwave, coffeemaker, etc.), when you design the interior of your house. Also, your Sims cannot prepare food on a table, so provide ample countertop space in the kitchen, or you may find them wandering into the bathroom to chop veggies on the counter (hair in the soup—yummy!).

Countertops

NuMica Kitchen Counter

Cost: §150

Motive: None

Tiled Counter

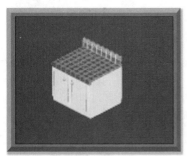

Cost: §250

Motive: None

Count Blanc Bathroom Counter

Cost: §400

Motive: None

"Barcelona" Outcurve Counter

Cost: §800

Motive: Room (2)

"Barcelona" Incurve Counter

Cost: §800

Motive: Room (2)

End Tables

Pinegulcher End Table

Cost: §40

Motive: None

Wicker Breeze End Table

Cost: §55

Motive: None

"Anywhere" End Table

Cost: §120

Motive: None

Imperious Island End Table

Cost: §135

Motive: None

Modern Mission End Table

Cost: §250

Motive: Room (1)

Sumpto End Table

Cost: §300

Motive: Room (1)

KinderStuff Nightstand

Cost: §75

Motive: None

Desks/Tables

Mesquite Desk/Table

Cost: §80

Motive: None

NuMica Folding Card Table

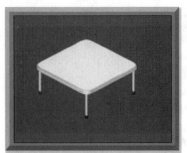

Cost: §95

Motive: None

"Colonial Legacy" Dining Table

Cost: §200

Motive: None

Backwoods Table by Survivall

Cost: §200

Motive: None

London "Cupertino" Collection Desk/Table

Cost: §220

Motive: None

London "Mesa" Dining Design

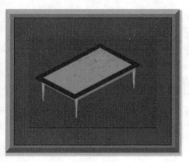

Cost: §450

Motive: Room (2)

The "Redmond" Desk/Table

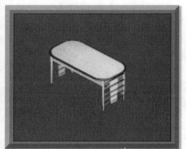

Cost: §800

Motive: Room (2)

Parisienne Dining Table

Cost: §1,200

Motive: Room (3)

Decorative

After the essential furnishings are in place, you can improve your Room score by adding decorative objects. Some items, such as the grandfather clock and aquarium, require regular maintenance, but most decorative items exist solely for your Sims' viewing pleasure. You might even get lucky and buy a painting or sculpture that increases in value. In addition to enhancing the Room score, the aquarium and fountain have Fun value.

Pink Flamingo

Cost: §12

Motive: Room (2)

African Violet

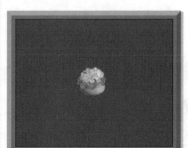

Cost: §30

Motive: Room (1)

Spider Plant

Cost: §35

Motive: Room (1)

Watercolor by J.M.E.

Cost: §75

Motive: Room (1)

"Roxana" Geranium

Cost: §45

Motive: Room (1)

Rubber Tree Plant

Cost: §120

Motive: Room (2)

"Tragic Clown" Painting

Cost: §45

Motive: Room (1)

Echinopsis maximus Cactus

Cost: §150

Motive: Room (2)

Jade Plant

Cost: §160

Motive: Room (2)

"Delusion de Grandeur"

Cost: §360

Motive: Room (2)

Poseidon's Adventure Aquarium

Cost: §200

Motive: Fun (1), Room (2)

"Fountain of Tranquility"

Cost: §700

Motives: Fun (1), Room (2)

"Bi-Polar" by Conner I.N.

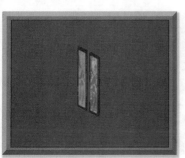

Cost: §240

Motive: Room (2)

Landscape #12,001 by Manny Kopees

Cost: §750

Motive: Room (3)

Bust of Athena by Klassick Repro. Inc.

Cost: §875

Motive: Room (3)

Portrait Grid by Payne A. Pitcher

Cost: §3,200

Motive: Room (8)

"Scylla and Charybdis"

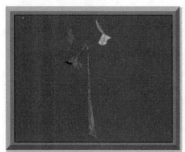

Cost: §1,450

Motive: Room (4)

Grandfather Clock

Cost: §3,500

Motive: Room (7)

Snails With Icicles in Nose

Cost: §2,140

Motive: Room (5)

Blue China Vase

Cost: §4,260

Motive: Room (7)

"Still Life, Drapery and Crumbs"

Cost: §7,600

Motive: Room (9)

"Large Black Slab" by ChiChi Smith

Cost: §12,648

Motive: Room (10)

Electronics

This game offers a veritable potpourri of high-tech gadgetry, ranging from potentially lifesaving items such as smoke detectors to nonessential purchases such as pinball games or virtual reality headsets. Beyond the critical electronics items—smoke detectors, telephone for receiving calls or calling services and friends, TV for cheap fun, and computer for finding a job—you should focus on items with group activity potential, especially if you like socializing and throwing parties.

TIP

Electronic items can break down on a regular basis, so it is a good idea to bone up on Mechanical Skills. Until you have a qualified fix-it Sim in the house, you'll be shelling out §50 an hour for a repairman.

FireBrand Smoke Detector

Cost: §50

Motive: None

Notes: Each detector covers one room. At the very least, place a detector in any room that has a stove or fireplace.

SimSafety IV Burglar Alarm

Cost: §250

Motive: None

Notes: An alarm unit covers one room, but an outside alarm covers an area within five tiles of the house. The police are called immediately when the alarm goes off.

SCTC BR-8 Standard Telephone

Cost: §50

Motive: None

Notes: This phone needs a surface, so it's less accessible. Best location is in the kitchen; stick with wall phones in the rest of the house.

SCTC Cordless Wall Phone

Cost: §75

Motive: None

Notes: Place these phones wherever your Sims spend a lot of time.

Urchineer Train Set by Rip Co.

Cost: §80

Motive: Fun (2)

Notes: Group activity; can only be used by kids.

Televisions

Buying a TV is the easiest way to put a little fun into your Sims' lives, and it is a group activity. You can maximize the effect by matching the program category with your Sim's personality, as noted in the following table.

PERSONALITY	FAVORITE TV SHOW
Active	Action
Grouchy (low nice)	Horror
Outgoing	Romance
Playful	Cartoon

Your TV will eventually break down, especially if you have a family of couch potatoes. Do not attempt to repair the TV unless your Sim has at least one Mechanical Skill point (three is even better). If your Sim doesn't have the proper training, poking around inside the TV will result in electrocution.

Monochrome TV

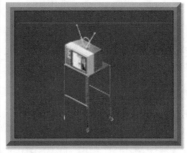

Cost: §85

Motive: Fun (2)

Notes: Strictly for tight budgets, but it gives your Sims a little mindless fun.

Trottco 27" Color Television B94U

Cost: §500

Motive: Fun (4)

Notes: A lazy Sim's favorite activity is watching TV.

Soma Plasma TV

Cost: §3,500

Motive: Fun (6), Room (2)

Notes: It's expensive, but it provides instant entertainment for a full house.

Stereos

Dancing to the music is a great group activity, especially for Sims with effervescent personalities (although it is perfectly acceptable to dance alone). When a Sim dances with a houseguest, it increases both their Fun and Social ratings. You can personalize *The Sims* by placing your own MP3 files in the Music/Stations directory.

"Down Wit Dat" Boom Box

Cost: §100

Motive: Fun (2)

Notes: An inexpensive way to start a party in your front yard.

Zimantz Component Hi-Fi Stereo

Cost: §650

Motive: Fun (3)

Notes: Perfect for your big party room.

Strings Theory Stereo

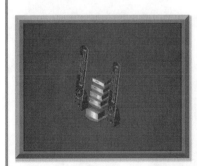

Cost: §2,550

Motives: Fun (5), Room (3)

Notes: The ultimate party machine, this is the only stereo that enhances your Room score.

Computers

A computer is a Sim's best tool for finding a job. The computer has three job postings every day, making it three times as productive as the newspaper employment ads. Aside from career search, the computer provides entertainment for the entire family, and it helps the kids keep their grades up (better chance of cash rewards from the grandparents). Playful and lazy Sims love the computer. However, if only serious Sims occupy your house, you can grab a newspaper and let the age of technology pass you by.

Moneywell Computer

Cost: §999

Motive: Fun (3), Study

Notes: All you need is a basic computer for job searching.

Microscotch Covetta Q628-1500JA

Cost: §1,800

Motive: Fun (5), Study

Notes: More power translates into better gaming.

The Brahma 2000

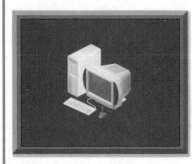

Cost: §2,800

Motive: Fun (7), Study

Notes: More than twice the fun of a basic computer.

Meet Marco

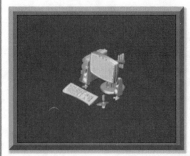

Cost: §6,500

Motive: Fun (9), Study

Notes: For Sim power users—the family will fight for playing time on this beast.

Games

OCD Systems SimRailRoad Town

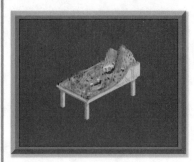

Cost: §955

Motive: Fun (4), Room (3)

Notes: You need a large area for this train table, but it is an excellent group activity and it gives a serious boost to your Room score.

"See Me, Feel Me" Pinball Machine

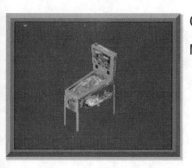

Cost: §1,800

Motive: Fun (5)

Notes: Build a big family room and add a pinball machine to keep your guests occupied for hours.

SSRI Virtual Reality Set

Cost: §2,300

Motive: Fun (7)

Notes: Playful Sims have been known to don VR glasses on their way to the bathroom (even with full bladders). For grins, wait until a Sim puts on the glasses, then immediately issue another command. The Sim head on the control panel will wear the glasses for the duration of your game.

Appliances

With the exception of the dishwasher and trash compactor, the Sim appliances are all devoted to the creation of food or java. At a bare minimum, you need refrigeration. However, if you want your Sims to eat like royalty, train at least one family member in the gentle art of cooking and provide that Sim with the latest in culinary tools.

Mr. Regular-Joe Coffee

Cost: §85

Motive: Bladder (-1), Energy (1)

Notes: Only adults can partake of the coffee rush. The effects are temporary, but sometimes it's the only way to get rolling.

Gagmia Simore Espresso Machine

Cost: §450

Motive: Bladder (-2), Energy (2), Fun (1)

Notes: If you want a morning jolt, espresso is the way to go. You'll fill your bladder twice as fast as with regular coffee, but it is a small price to pay for more energy and a splash of fun.

Brand Name Toaster Oven

Cost: §100

Motive: Hunger (1)

Notes: This little roaster is better at starting fires than cooking food. Improve your Cooking Skills and buy a real oven. Until then, use a microwave.

Positive Potential Microwave

Cost: §250

Motive: Hunger (2)

Notes: You can warm up your food without burning the house down.

Dialectric Free Standing Range

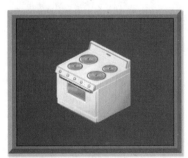

Cost: §400

Motive: Hunger (5)

Notes: After raising your Cooking Skills to three or above, you can create nutritious (and satisfying) meals on this stove.

The "Pyrotorre" Gas Range

Cost: §1,000

Motive: Hunger (7)

Notes: A skilled chef can create works of art on this stove.

NOTE

Although an expensive stove enhances your Sim meals, it is only one of three steps in the cooking process. To maximize the potential of your stove, you need an excellent refrigerator for storage, and a food processor for efficient preparation.

Wild Bill THX-451 Barbecue

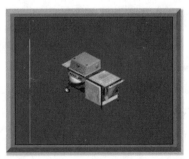

Cost: §350

Motive: Hunger (4)

Notes: Only experienced adult chefs should fire up the barbecue. Be careful not to position the grill near flammable items.

XLR8R Food Processor

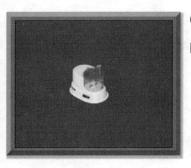

Cost: §220

Motive: Hunger (2)

Notes: A food processor speeds up meal preparation and enhances food quality.

Junk Genie Trash Compactor

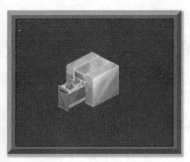

Cost: §375

Motive: None

Notes: A compactor holds more garbage than a trash can, and even when it is full, it will not degrade the Room rating because the trash is concealed.

Dish Duster Deluxe

Cost: §550

Motive: Dirty dishes lower your Room score.

Notes: Kids can't use the dishwasher, but it still cuts cleanup time considerably, and the countertop can be used for placing other items (sorry, no eating allowed).

Fuzzy Logic Dishwasher

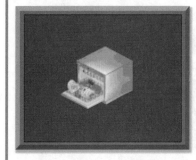

Cost: §950

Motive: Dirty dishes lower your Room score.

Notes: The Cadillac of dishwashers cleans up kitchen messes in a snap. This model has fewer breakdowns than the Dish Duster.

Llamark Refrigerator

Cost: §600

Motive: Hunger (6)

Notes: This model is sufficient while your Sims are building up their Cooking Skills.

Porcina Refrigerator Model P1g-S

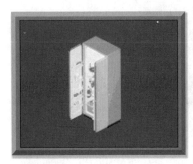

Cost: §1,200

Motive: Hunger (7)

Notes: This model produces more satisfying food for your Sims.

Freeze Secret Refrigerator

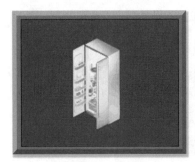

Cost: §2,500

Motive: Hunger (8)

Notes: The best place to store your food. When it's matched with a food processor, gas stove, and an experienced chef, your Sims will be licking their lips.

Plumbing

Sims can't carry buckets to the well for their weekly bath, and the outhouse hasn't worked in years, so install various plumbing objects to maintain a clean, healthy environment. Of course, not every plumbing object is essential, but you can't beat a relaxing hour in the hot tub with a few of your closest friends (or casual acquaintances).

Hydronomic Kitchen Sink

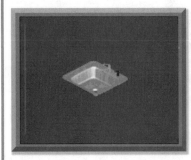

Cost: §250

Motive: Hygiene (2)

Notes: Without it the Sims would be washing dishes in the bathroom.

Epikouros Kitchen Sink

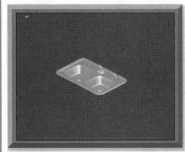

Cost: §500

Motive: Hygiene (3)

Notes: It's twice as big as the single, but a dishwasher is a better investment.

"Andersonville" Pedestal Sink

Cost: §400

Motive: Hygiene (2)

Notes: Neat Sims like to wash their hands after using the toilet.

Hygeia-O-Matic Toilet

Cost: §300

Motive: Bladder (8)

Notes: Hey, your only other option is the floor.

Flush Force 5 XLT

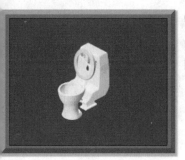

Cost: §1,200

Motives: Comfort (4), Bladder (8)

Notes: Your Sims can't go to the ballpark to get a good seat, but they can sit in a lap of luxury in the bathroom.

SpaceMiser Shower

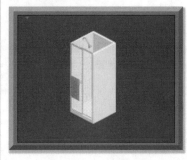

Cost: §650

Motive: Hygiene (6)

Notes: This is basic equipment in a Sims bathroom. One Sim can shower at a time, and the neat ones tend to linger longer than the sloppy ones. Sims are generally shy if they are not in love with a housemate, so you may need more than one shower (and bathroom) to prevent a traffic jam in the bathroom.

Justa Bathtub

Cost: §800

Motives: Comfort (3), Hygiene (6)

Notes: Your Sims get a double benefit from a relaxing bath when they have a little extra time.

Sani-Queen Bathtub

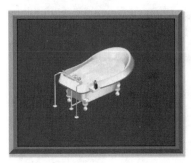

Cost: §1,500

Motives: Comfort (5), Hygiene (8)

Notes: Almost twice the price, but the added Comfort and Hygiene points are worth it.

Hydrothera Bathtub

Cost: §3,200

Motives: Comfort (8), Hygiene (10)

Notes: The most fun a Sim can have alone. Save your Simoleans, buy it, and listen to sounds of relaxation.

WhirlWizard Hot Tub

Cost: §6,500

Motives: Comfort (6), Hygiene (2), Fun (2)

Notes: Up to four adult Sims can relax, mingle, and begin lasting relationships in the hot tub.

Lighting

Sims love natural light, so make sure the sun shines through your windows from every direction. And, when the sun goes down, your Sims need plenty of lighting on the walls, floors, and tables to illuminate their world until bedtime. Although only three lamps listed below have direct impact on the Room score, all of the lamps have a collective effect when spread evenly throughout the home. Pay special attention to key activity areas in the kitchen, family room, bedrooms, and of course, the bathroom.

CAUTION

Lamp bulbs burn out with use, and they must be replaced. Sims can replace their own bulbs, but without Mechanical Skills, they run the risk of electrocution. Hiring a repairman is another option, but at §50 per hour, this can be very costly.

Table Lamps

Bottle Lamp

Cost: §25

Motive: None

Love n' Haight Lava Lamp

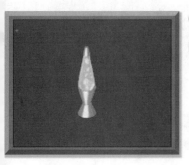

Cost: §80

Motive: Room (2)

Ceramiche Table Lamp

Cost: §85

Motive: None

Elite Reflections Chrome Lamp

Cost: §180

Motive: None

SC Electric Co. Antique Lamp

Cost: §300

Motive: Room (1)

Floor Lamps

Halogen Heaven Lamp by Contempto

Cost: §50

Motive: None

Lumpen Lumeniat Floor Lamp

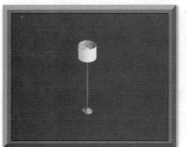

Cost: §100

Motive: None

Torchosteronne Floor Lamp

Cost: §350

Motive: Room (1)

Top Brass Sconce

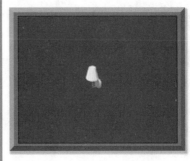

Cost: §110

Motive: None

Wall Lamps

White Globe Sconce

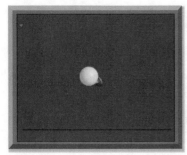

Cost: §35

Motive: None

Blue Plate Special Sconce

Cost: §135

Motive: None

Outside Lamp

Garden Lamp (Outdoor Use Only)

Cost: §50

Motive: None

Oval Glass Sconce

Cost: §85

Motive: None

Miscellaneous

We're down to the objects that are hard to fit into a category—everything from bookcases to beverage bars. Don't make the mistake of ignoring these items because you think they're luxuries; your Sim's life would be extremely difficult without a trash can, alarm clock, and bookcase. Plus, if you want to improve your Sim's Charisma and Body ratings, you'll need a mirror and exercise machine. So, once you install the basic objects in your house, look to the Miscellaneous category for objects that take your Sim's lifestyle to the next level.

SnoozMore Alarm Clock

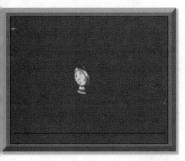

Cost: §30

Motive: None

Notes: After you set the clock, it will ring two hours before the carpool arrives for every working Sim in your house.

Trash Can

Cost: §30

Motive: None

Notes: Without a place to put trash, your Sim house will become a fly-infested hovel.

Magical Mystery Toy Box

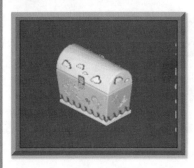

Cost: §50

Motive: Fun (2)

Notes: A good entertainment alternative if your kids are getting bleary-eyed in front of the computer.

Narcisco Wall Mirror

Cost: §100

Motive: Improves Charisma

Notes: Adults can Practice speech in front of the mirror to improve their Charisma.

Medicine Cabinet

Cost: §125

Motive: Hygiene (1), Improves Charisma

Notes: Your Sims can Practice speech in the bathroom and improve their Hygiene at the same time.

Narcisco Floor Mirror

Cost: §150

Motive: Improves Charisma

Notes: Place this mirror anywhere to practice Charisma without locking other Sims out of the bathroom.

Will Lloyd Wright Doll House

Cost: §180

Motive: Fun (2)

Notes: An engaging group activity for kids and adults.

Cheap Pine Bookcase

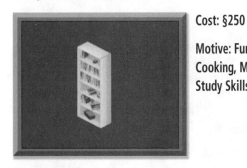

Cost: §250

Motive: Fun (1), Improve Cooking, Mechanical, and Study Skills

Notes: Reading books is the best way to prevent premature death from fires or electrocution.

"Dimanche" Folding Easel

Cost: §250

Motive: Fun (2), Improves Creativity

Notes: With practice, a Sim can improve Creativity, and eventually sell a picture for up to §166.

Pinegulcher Dresser

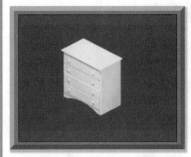

Cost: §250

Motive: None

Notes: A Sim can change into various formal, work, and leisure outfits, and even acquire a new body type.

Kinderstuff Dresser

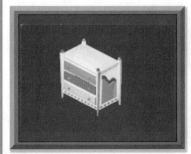

Cost: §300

Motive: None

Notes: Kids like to dress up too!

Amishim Bookcase

Cost: §500

Motive: Fun (2), Improves Cooking, Mechanical, and Study Skills

Notes: This expensive bookcase awards Skill points at the same rate as the cheaper one.

Chuck Matewell Chess Set

Cost: §500

Motive: Fun (2), Improves Logic

Notes: Serious Sims gain the most Fun points by playing, and any two Sims can improve Logic by playing each other.

Traditional Oak Armoire

Cost: §550

Motive: Room (1)

Notes: This dresser allows your Sim to change clothes (body skins). The choices vary, depending upon the Sim's current outfit.

SuperDoop Basketball Hoop

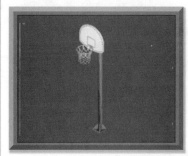

Cost: §650

Motive: Fun (4)

Notes: Active Sims love to play hoops, and any visitor is welcome to join the fun. A Sim with higher Body points performs better on the court.

"Exerto" Benchpress Exercise Machine

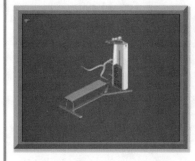

Cost: §700

Motive: Improves Body

Notes: Adult Sims can bulk up their Body points with exercise sessions.

Bachman Wood Beverage Bar

Cost: §800

Motive: Hunger (1), Fun (3), Room (2)

Notes: Every drink lowers the Bladder score, but adult Sims like to make drinks for themselves and friends. Kids can grab a soda from the fridge.

Libri di Regina Bookcase

Cost: §900

Motive: Fun (3), Improves Cooking, Mechanical, and Study Skills

Notes: This stylish bookcase is perfect for a swanky Sim pad, but it still imparts Skill points at the same rate as the pine model.

Antique Armoire

Cost: §1,200

Motive: Room (2)

Notes: A more expensive version of the cheaper armoire, but it adds twice as many Room points.

The Funinator Deluxe

Cost: §1,200

Motive: Fun (5)

Notes: When the house is swarming with kids, send them outside to raise their Fun bar and burn some energy.

Chimeway & Daughters Piano

Cost: §3,500

Motive: Fun (4), Room (3), Improves Creativity

Notes: The most creative Sims will produce more beautiful music. The better the music, the greater the chance that listeners will like it. If a listener does not like the music, both Sims' Relationship scores will deteriorate.

Aristoscratch Pool Table

Cost: §4,200

Motive: Fun (6)

Notes: Up to two Sims use the table at the same time. Make sure that you allow enough room for Sims to get to the table and walk around it during play.

CHAPTER 7:
ALL IN THE FAMILY

Introduction

Up to this point, we've covered the mechanics of *The Sims*. By now you should be familiar with creating families, building houses, buying objects, and getting jobs; and you should have considerable insight into how a Sim thinks and acts. Now, let's put it all together and join several Sim households in action. In this chapter we introduce you to working Sims families, ranging from one-Sim homes to larger households with kids and babies. Finally, we take an in-depth look at one of the toughest challenges in *The Sims*: building positive (and long-lasting) Relationships.

You Can Make It Alone

The biggest difficulty in being a bachelor is that you have to do everything yourself (sounds like real life, doesn't it?). You'll need to cook, clean, and improve your Skills, while at the same time keep up with a work schedule and satisfy your personal Motives. There's always time for Fun, and a good sofa or easy chair will provide a measure of Comfort. However, it's impossible to socialize while at work, and you will be frustrated watching neighbors drop by during the day and then leave when no one answers the door.

The Single Sim's Career

As a lone Sim you must choose a job that has decent hours and light friendship demands. This leaves a Military career as your only option. At most levels you work a six-hour day, and you won't need a single friend for the first five levels. A promotion to Level 6 requires one friend, but that can be established after you refine your schedule.

Designing a Bachelor Pad

There are several considerations when designing and furnishing a house for one Sim. Review the following checklist before you place your first wall stake.

Fig. 7-1. It's hardly the lap of luxury, but you have everything you need to get a job, keep your sanity, and learn how to cook.

- **Keep your house small, and place the front door close to the street. This allows you to milk a few extra minutes out of every morning before meeting the car pool.**

- **The interior should include a bedroom, bathroom, and living room. Rather than add a family room, use an outside patio area for Fun objects and an exercise machine. A Military career requires an ever-increasing number of Body Skill points.**

- **Install only enough counter space to place a food processor and prepare your meals. This leaves more space for a table and chairs. Buy at least two chairs so that you can socialize with a friend while sharing a meal.**

- **Without the space or the budget to buy expensive sofas or recliners, get a top-of-the-line bed, which enables your Sim to get by on fewer hours of sleep. Buy an inexpensive nightstand for an alarm clock, and add a few wall lights to boost your Room score.**

- **You'll need a computer for your job search, but keep in mind that you can return it within 24 Sim-hours for a full refund. Find your Military job and then pack up the PC.**

- **Buy an expensive refrigerator to maximize the quality of your food, but don't bother with a stove until your Sim learns how to cook.**
- **Because of your career, there's no need to socialize until you are up for promotion to Level 6, so don't waste money on living room chairs or an expensive sofa. A cheap TV will provide enough Fun for now.**

Leaving the Single Life

Eventually you will tire of the solitary lifestyle, which, thanks to the romantic tendencies of most Sims, is not a problem. The first step is friendship. After the Relationship bar tops 70, your Sim needs to lay on the romance, with plenty of kissing and hugging. Eventually, the Propose option will appear on the menu.

Fig. 7-2. The kissin' and huggin' pays off; now it's time to pop the question.

A marriage proposal can only take place in the home of the proposer, so set the mood (you know, empty your Bladder somewhere other than on the floor, clean up yesterday's dishes, and hide those overdue bills). After accepting the proposal, your new spouse moves into your place, along with a good job (a good thing) and plenty of money (a really good thing). But, proposing does not guarantee a positive response. For example, a Sim will never accept the proposal on an empty stomach, so you might want to eat dinner first.

Fig. 7-3. "We're alone, the time is perfect, and I've got grass stains on my knee."

Fig. 7-4. "Nope, sorry, I can't marry you on an empty stomach. Besides, your current lover is hiding in the bushes."

Keep in mind that you have to create potential mates, because the game won't provide them. You might as well choose compatible personalities, and it doesn't hurt to spend some time on career development. Remember that another Sim can also propose to you in his or her house; so unless you want to change residences, hold the romantic interludes at your place.

NOTE

After marriage, your Sim will still share a bed with any other Sim with a high enough Friendship score (over 70), so don't be surprised if your Sim ends up on the couch when his buddy beats him to the sack.

Fig. 7-5. When two Sims decide to get married, they change clothes and complete the ceremony within seconds.

A three-way relationship makes it easier to have babies. Not only are there additional combinations for procreation, but you can also have one of the working adults take a night job, so there is a caregiver for the baby during the day. Even with staggered schedules, there will be at least one sleepless Sim until the baby matures, so don't get too complacent with this arrangement.

Interestingly, if your future spouse already has children, and at least one adult still resides in his or her original house, the kids stay. So, your new spouse arrives with job and bank account intact, sans kids. What a deal!

That isn't the only unusual aspect of married life in SimsVille. Marriage is not sacred here, at least not in the legal sense. A Sim can have multiple mates all living under the same roof, as pictured in figure 7-6. The interpersonal dynamics can sometimes get a little dicey, but it's workable, and the extra income is great!

Married, with Children

After your Sims promise undying love and devotion to each other (or, at least until the next promotion), it's time to have a baby. Actually, your Sims can live together for years without having children, but if they do, you'll be missing one of the *The Sims*' most vexing experiences.

Conception

The exercise of making a baby is similar to the steps taken to activate the marriage Proposal option. First, get a male and female Sim together, and then concentrate on strengthening their relationship. When both Sims are obviously enjoying each other's company, lay on the hugs and kisses. Keep smooching until you receive the option to have a baby, as pictured in figure 7-7.

Fig. 7-6. After the wedding, our Sim bride goes to bed with her former boyfriend.

Fig. 7-7. A little bundle of joy is just a click away.

If you answer yes, a bassinet appears almost instantly, amid an explosion of dandelions. The happy couple celebrates the new arrival, then they quickly go back to their daily routine. This baby thing is a snap. Well, not exactly.

Fig. 7-8. Yippee! It's a boy!

In short order, the little bundle of joy starts screaming. A Sim will eventually respond to the cries, but rather than wait, get someone to the baby immediately. Clicking on the bassinet reveals three options: Feed, Play, or Sing. When in doubt, Feed the baby, but be prepared to come right back with Play or Sing when the baby starts wailing again.

Fig. 7-9. Kids do a great job entertaining the baby during one of its frequent crying sessions.

This mayhem continues for three Sim days, during which time the household will be in an uproar. Forget about getting eight hours of beauty sleep. Designate one Sim as primary caregiver, preferably one who does not work, because the baby's cries wake any Sim in the room. The first day is nonstop crying. By the second day, the baby sleeps for a few hours at a time; take advantage of the break and send the caregiver to bed. As long as you stay responsive, the baby evolves into a runny-nosed kid, and the family can get back to normal. However, if you spend too much time in the hot tub and not enough time with the baby, a social service worker will march into your house and take the baby, as pictured in figure 7-10. You'll only receive one warning, so don't take this responsibility lightly.

Fig. 7-10. We hardly knew the little tyke!

NOTE

The bassinet appears near the spot where your Sims made the decision to have a baby. Although the Sims cannot move the bassinet, you can use the Hand Tool to move it. Pick a location that is isolated from other sleeping areas, so the disturbance is kept to a minimum.

Building and Maintaining Healthy Relationships

Gathering an ever-increasing number of friends is critical for career advancement, especially at the higher levels. It is also your Sims' only way to build up their Social scores and fend off frequent bouts of depression. In this section we outline the steps required for finding potential friends, building up positive feelings, and then maintaining healthy relationships.

Talk Is Cheap

The easiest way to make friends is often overlooked, because it is uneventful compared to other social events. However, you can almost always initiate a conversation between Sims (regardless of their Friendship scores), and keep it going for a very long time. During this benign exchange of thought balloons, you can usually nudge the Friendship score in a positive direction. When starting from 0 it takes a few encounters to get over 50 (true friendship), but once you reach this threshold, the action picks up considerably. Our newly married Sims went from a score of 64 to a marriage proposal in one evening. Although the woman eventually declined because her stomach was growling, she proposed the next day and the marriage was consummated.

Fig. 7-11. Keep talking and your Friendship score will grow.

Finding Time to Socialize

After your Sim starts working, it's difficult to find time to call other Sims and arrange meetings. Mornings are worst, although you have more options if your neighborhood has several non-working Sims. Your best bet is to start socializing right after coming home from work. Take care of personal needs first—Hygiene and Bladder—and then "Serve Dinner." Don't let a bad chef get near the stove; you can't afford to waste time putting out a fire or your guests will leave. With a counter full of food, your friends head straight for the kitchen, where you can chat over a plate of Sim-grub and then plan the rest of your evening.

Positive Social Events

After everyone is finished eating, take a little time for pleasant conversation. In the case of the female Sims pictured in figure 7-11, there is a lot of fence mending to accomplish, because one just stole the other's love interest. But, Sims are generally forgiving, and a quarrel can be mended with a few drinks, a game of pool, or a long soak in the hot tub.

Ideally, your house has an entertainment room with group activity items such as a pool table, stereo, or beverage bar. After you get everyone into the room, keep them busy with a string of activities. Even our former lovers can't resist a dance when the music starts playing, as pictured in figure 7-12.

Fig. 7-12. Our Sim guy is enjoying this dance with his former girlfriend, although his current wife will probably slap him when the music stops playing (if she can stay awake long enough).

CAUTION

Avoid close activities such as dancing, hugging, etc. when the current spouse or love interest is in the room. When the dance was over (figure 7-12), our Sim wife did indeed slap her new husband, causing her recently mended Relationship score with the other woman to drop from +14 to –7.

CAUTION

Visiting Sims generally hang around until 1:00 a.m. or later, which is undoubtedly past your bedtime. Direct your Sims to bed at the appropriate time, or they may feel compelled to hang out with their guests until well past midnight, as pictured in figure 7-14.

Fig. 7-14. Our host Sim is still cleaning up dishes when he should be asleep.

One of the most difficult aspects of entertaining in the evening is keeping the host from falling asleep on the floor. After a hard day's work, most Sims begin nodding out around 10:00 p.m. You can squeeze a little extra time out of the evening if they take a short nap after coming home from work. Be prepared for a grouchy Sim in the morning (figure 7-13) if the evening's festivities stretch too far into the night.

Fig. 7-13. Our tired party girl hurries off to the car pool without a shower—not a good way to impress her superiors.

TIP

After your guests arrive, you need to micromanage your Sims so they don't go off and take care of their own needs. Obviously, you must pay attention to a full Bladder, but you can delay other actions by redirecting your Sims to group activities. Break up the party when your Sims are teetering on the edge of exhaustion or they'll fall asleep on the floor.

Stockpiling Potential Friends

When your career advances to the top promotion level, you need more than 10 friends in every career except the Military. Hence, it's a good idea to create a few additional families early in the game, and you might want to fill one house with the maximum of eight Sims to dramatically increase your pool.

Visitors Coming and Going

The following tables include important information on how and why visitors do the things they do. You may not be able to directly control your guests' actions, but at least you won't take it personally when they decide to split.

Visitors' Starting Motives

MOTIVE	STARTING VALUE
Bladder	0 to 30
Comfort	30 to 70
Energy	35
Fun	-20 to 20
Hunger	-30 to -20
Hygiene	90
Social	-50 to -40

In a perfect Sim-world, visitors leave your house just past 1:00 a.m. However if one of their Motives falls into the danger zone, they will depart earlier. When this happens, the Sim's thought balloon reveals a reason for the early exit.

Visitors' Leaving Motives

MOTIVE	DROPS BELOW THIS VALUE
Bladder	-90
Comfort	-70
Energy	-80
Fun	-55
Hunger	-50
Hygiene	-70
Mood	-75
Room	-100
Social	-85

Guest Activities

There are three types of visitor activities: those initiated by a family member, shared activities, and autonomous activities where guests are on their own. The following sections and tables describe each type.

Activities Initiated by Family Member

One of the Sims under your control must prepare food or turn on the TV before visitors can join in. Turning on the TV takes a second, but you need a little prep time for a meal. It's a good idea to begin meal preparation immediately after inviting friends over.

Shared Activities

A Sim can start any of the following activities and then invite the participation of a guest.

OBJECT	VISITORS' INVOLVEMENT
Basketball Hoop	Join
Chess	Join
Dollhouse	Watch
Hot Tub	Join
Pinball Machine	Join
Play Structure	Join
Piano	Watch
Pool Table	Join
Stereo	Join, Dance
Train Set	Watch

Autonomous Activities

Visiting Sims can begin any of the following activities on their own.

Visitors' Autonomous Activities

OBJECT	AUTONOMOUS ACTION
Aquarium	Watch Fish
Baby	Play
Bar	Have a Drink
Chair	Sit
Chair (Recliner)	Sit
Coffee (Espresso Machine)	Drink Espresso
Coffeemaker	Drink Coffee
Fire	Panic
Flamingo	View
Fountain	Play
Lava Lamp	View
Painting	View
Pool	Swim
Pool Diving Board	Dive In
Pool Ladder	Get In/Out
Sculpture	View
Sink	Wash Hands
Sofa	Sit
Toilet	Use, Flush
Tombstone/Urn	Mourn
Toy Box	Play
Trash Can (Inside)	Dispose

Social Interactions

The results of various interactions are best learned by experience because of the individual personality traits that come into play. However, it helps to have an idea what each action may produce. The following table offers notes on each interaction.

INTERACTION	DESCRIPTION
Back Rub	When well-received, it is a good transition into kissing and hugging, but the Relationship score should already be over 50.
Brag	This is what mean Sims do to your Sim. Don't use it, unless you want to ruin a good friendship.
Compliment	Generally positive, but you should withhold compliments until your Relationship score is above 15.
Dance	Great activity between friends (40+), but it almost always causes a jealous reaction from a jilted lover.
Entertain	A somewhat goofy activity, but it usually works well with other Playful Sims.
Fight	Don't do it (unless you know you can take the other Sim!).
Flirt	A great way to boost a strong Relationship (70+) into the serious zone, but watch your back. Flirting usually triggers a jealous reaction from significant others.
Give Gift	A benign way to say you like the other Sim, or that you're sorry for acting like an idiot at the last party; best used with 40+ Relationship scores.
Hug	This one's always fun if the hug-ee's Relationship score is +60; a good transition to kisses, and then a marriage proposal.
Joke	Good between casual friends (+15) who are both Playful.
Kiss	The relationship is heating up, but if a jealous ex or current lover is in the vicinity, someone could get slapped.
Talk	The starting point of every friendship.
Tease	Why bother, unless you don't like the other Sim.
Tickle	Not as positive as it might seem, but Playful Sims are definitely more receptive.

CHAPTER 8:
A DAY IN THE LIFE

Introduction

Now, it's time to turn on our Sim-Cam and follow a few of our families as they handle the ups and downs of Sim life. In this chapter we switch to a scrapbook format, with screenshots of our Sims in interesting—and sometimes compromising—situations. Admittedly, we coaxed our Sims into some of these dilemmas. But it's all in fun, and we think it's the best way for you to get a feel for this amazing game.

As the Sim Turns

Our third adult roommate, Mortimer, just returned home from his night shift, so for now, his needs are secondary. We put him to work mopping the kitchen floor (the dishwasher broke last night, but everyone was falling asleep, so we figured it would keep until morning).

Five o'clock wakeup call is not pretty. Even with full Energy bars, your Sims can be a little cranky, but don't give them any slack. Get the best chef into the kitchen pronto, to serve Breakfast for everyone in the house.

Before we are accused of being sexist, we should explain that the only reason Bella is cooking for everyone is that she is the most experienced chef. If Mark turns on the stove, chances are the kitchen will burn down. We promise to boost his Cooking Skills at the first opportunity.

Switching to Zoomed Out view is a good way to manage the household early in the morning. This way you can quickly target important tasks for completion before the car pool arrives.

Mark is, well, busy at the moment. It's too bad he doesn't gain Energy points for sitting on the toilet, because he stayed up much too late last night. A good breakfast helps, but getting through the day won't be easy, and he can forget about any promotions thanks to his sub-par mood.

It's a nice family breakfast with husband Mortimer on the left, wife Bella on the right, and Bella's ex-boyfriend Mark in the middle. However, there isn't much time for chitchat, because the car pool has arrived, and it will leave at a few minutes past nine.

After canceling his thoughts about sleeping, we click on Mark's car pool. He changes clothes faster than Superman and sprints to his ride in the nick of time. Have a nice day, Mark!

Bella is on her way to the car pool and we have about a half hour to get Mark in gear, which may be a problem due to his low Energy rating. Unfortunately, Bella's Hygiene leaves much to be desired. We make a mental note to get her into the shower before bedtime tonight so she'll be fresh as a daisy in the mornin).

Poor Mortimer! We've been so focused on getting Bella and Mark to work, we didn't notice that the poor slob is asleep on his feet! We need to wake him up (he'll be so happy), and send him to bed.

Uh-oh, big time problem with Mark. He's standing in the kitchen in his pajamas, in a catatonic state. With only a half hour to get to the car pool, we need to shake him up a little and point him to the door.

We receive a reminder that Mortimer's car pool arrives at 4:00 p.m. Unfortunately we forgot to set his alarm, and his Hygiene and Bladder bars have gone south, so we need to wake him up soon. Fortunately, he ate before bedtime, so he can probably get by without a big meal.

Mortimer is up and he's not happy. With the amount of time remaining before his car pool shows up, he can empty his bladder and get in half a shower before racing out the door.

Mark is well rested, so he can fend for himself this morning. He steps into the shower as the car pool arrives, so he has almost one hour to get ready. But, while in the shower, he decides to take the day off and join Bella.

With Mortimer out of the house, we can concentrate on Bella and Mark, who have both arrived home from work. Mark socialized a little too much the night before, so he went straight to bed without any prompting.

The three housemates share a pleasant breakfast together. Perhaps they have finally buried the hatchet after the Mortimer-Bella-Mark thing. We can only hope.

Mortimer arrives home at 1:00 a.m.. After a bathroom break and quick shower, we send him straight to bed so he can party with Bella tomorrow, who has decided to take the day off.

Mark grabs the phone to invite a friend over, but before he can dial, a local radio station calls with great news. He just won §550 in a promotion!

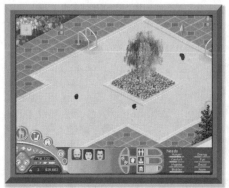

Mark calls a friend, who says he'll be right over. While Mark changes into his Speedo, Mortimer, Jeff, and Bella enjoy a dip in the pool. That's right, Mortimer missed his car pool, too. It's a day off (without pay) for the entire house!

After dinner, Jeff heads for home. Bella and Mark retreat to the den, where Bella rubs Mark's back.

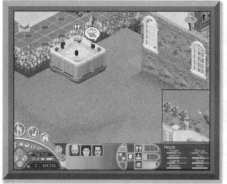

It's on to the hot tub for a long, relaxing soak. Comfort, Hygiene, Social, and Fun scores are soaring. It's too bad we have to eat and empty our Bladders or we'd never leave!

One good rub deserves a hug, as things suddenly heat up between the former lovers.

Everyone will be hungry after the swim and soak, so Bella hops out to make dinner. Soon, everyone grabs a plate and starts discussing what life will be like when they are all unemployed. Everyone, that is, except Mortimer, who prefers standing.

Mortimer takes one look at the lip-locked Sims and heads straight for the bar.

After a couple of adult beverages, Mortimer follows the lovers into the hallway where they are still groping each other like teenagers on prom night.

Mortimer shows his frustration by slapping Mark across the cheek (he's such an animal). Bella is disgusted and goes upstairs to bed.

One slap turns to another and seven hours later, Mortimer and Mark are still duking it out.

Bella drives off to work while our two Sim-Neanderthals take their fight to the bathroom.

What will become of our star-crossed lovers?

Will Bella leave Mortimer and go back to Mark?

Will Mark feel guilty about wrecking Mortimer's marriage, and move in with the Newbies?

Will Bella reveal what she and Jeff were really doing in the hot tub?

Who will clean up the bathroom?

For the answers to these burning questions, stay tuned for the next episode of...*As the Sim Turns.*

Life with the Pleasants

Jeff experiences the joys of working a night shift—cleaning up his family's dinner dishes...

...and taking out the trash at four in the morning.

Skeeter misses one too many days of school and gets the bad news—he's on his way to military school, never to be seen again.

Everyone is asleep, so Jeff takes an opportunity to practice his Charisma in front of the bathroom mirror. Unfortunately for Jeff, the walking dead also take this opportunity to float through the mirror and scare the •&$%$# out of him.

Although his icon has already disappeared from the control panel, Skeeter enjoys one last breakfast before he is exiled from the game.

Like all kids, Daniel and Skeeter can only make snacks on their own, so someone must serve their breakfast before school.

Not wanting to follow in his brother's footsteps, Daniel hits the books and improves his grades.

Hmmm. Which pile should I pay first, the red one or the yellow one? Get a clue, Jeff—if you don't pay the red ones, they'll repossess your furniture!

Pity the Poor Bachelor

With garbage a foot thick on the floor of his house, our bachelor decides to stay outside and entertain a new lady friend with his juggling act.

The Maid should get riot pay for all the garbage this family leaves on the floor!

"Wow, she really likes me! Maybe she won't notice the garbage if I invite her inside."

Maids are limited to cleaning up Sim-messes, but that frees up the family to take care of other important needs, like advancing their skills. Diane Pleasant takes a break to bone up on her Mechanical Skills. Perhaps she can fix the dishwasher and save §50-an-hour repair bills.

"I really like you Bella, so I got you a pair of basketball shoes!"

Bachelors on a fixed budget can have a difficult time having fun. A basketball hoop in the back yard is a good investment, and if you can find a Playful friend, it's a cheap date, too.

"Excuse me, son, could you please move out of the fire so I can extinguish it?"

Kids Are People, Too

Armed with a new gas stove and absolutely no cooking ability, this bachelor decides to flame-broil the kitchen.

Toy boxes are small and relatively inexpensive. If they are placed in the bedroom, your kids can sneak in a little Fun time before school.

Whew, the fireman is here to put out the fire. There's only one problem: he can't get into the house because our hero is standing in front of the stove, which happens to be next to the door. We understand that the bachelor's quarters are tight, but it's probably not a good idea to put the stove next to the front door. By the time the fireman makes his way to the back door, your bachelor could be toast.

Children have fewer inhibitions, but they still don't like to use the bathroom in front of the Maid or their siblings.

Skeeter and Matthew enjoy a little Social and Fun time playing with their railroad town.

Left to their own devices, kids often stay up long past the time their parents hit the sack. In fact, even with Free Will activated, parents feel no responsibility for getting their children to bed early. So, if you forget to send the kids to bed, get ready for some serious tantrums in the morning.

Skillful Sims

An exercise machine is the obvious choice for improving a Sim's Body Skill, but if you can keep your Sims in the pool, they'll increase Body scores even faster, and boost Fun at the same time.

Unlike the railroad, the pinball machine is a solo activity.

Unlike adults, who need toys for their playtime, kids can play with each other.

Sometimes it can be hard to get your Sims to slow down long enough for serious Skill enhancement, especially if it means sitting down to read. The solution is simple: Place two comfortable chairs close to the bookcase, and give each Sim different Skill assignments. Remember that you only need one Cooking expert and one Mechanical expert in the same house. Divide reading assignments appropriately to bring their Skills quickly up to speed.

You might be concerned about an adult male who stands for hours in front of a full-length mirror in his Speedo. However, it makes sense to place a mirror in the family room for easier access. This way, your Sims won't tie up the bathroom practicing Charisma in the mirror over the sink.

Increasing the Creativity Skill through painting has an added bonus—the ability to sell your painting. But, don't get too excited; a bad painting fetches only §1 on the open market.

With minimal Mechanical Skill, repairing this shower seems to take forever, and all the while, Mark's Comfort and Energy scores are dropping. Maybe a Repairman is worth the price until Mark earns a few more Mechanical points.

As the Sim Turns: Part Two

As we return to our Sim soap, Mortimer has just returned from another night shift, and after a light snack, he decides to take an early morning swim thinking that Mark and Bella are busy getting ready for work. After swimming a few laps, he is ready to go to bed, but wait...where is the ladder?

"I can't get out of the pool!" says Mortimer, frantically. "I'll just tread water for a while until Mark or Bella come out. If I can just...keep...going...getting tired...so tired...."

Mark and Bella finally come outside, but it's too late. Poor Mortimer, exhausted and confused, has already dropped like a stone to the bottom of the pool.

After Mortimer's body is removed from the pool, a tombstone is erected on the spot where the ladder used to be. If Mortimer were still here, he would have appreciated the humor...maybe not

After getting over the initial shock, Mark and Bella grieve at the site where their "friend" died.

Then, they console each other further...with a dance?

"O.K., enough grieving," says Bella, as she tells Mark a real knee-slapper.

Thinking the time is right (and that they have carried on the charade long enough), Mark pulls Bella close for a kiss. But, much to Mark's surprise, Bella suddenly cools and pushes him away.

What is this strange turn of events?

Did Bella entice Mark into helping her solve the "Mortimer" problem, only to leave him in the lurch?

Find the answers on the next episode of *As the Sim Turns*, **on a computer near you!**

After some welcome comic relief, the two mourners console each other with a supportive hug. Right.

Sims in the Kitchen

In the Motives chapter, we provided a basic explanation of how Sims satisfy their Hunger score. As you know by now, food is readily available in the refrigerator, 24 hours a Sim-day. The supply is endless, and you never have to go to the market. However, the difference between what is in the refrigerator and what a Sim actually eats lies in the preparation. The following screens take you through the various options available to a Sim chef, and the table at the end of this chapter explains how the different appliances and countertops modify the quality of each meal.

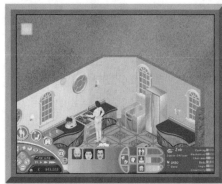

After processing the food, Bella throws it in a pot and works her magic. Two more modifier are at work here: Bella's Cooking Skill and the special features of the Pyrotorre Gas Range.

The snack, a §5 bag of chips, is the lowest item on the Sim food chain. It's better than nothing when your Sim is racing around getting ready for the car pool, but it barely nudges the Hunger bar.

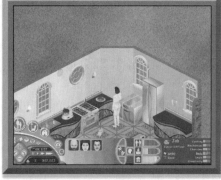

When the meal is finished, Bella places a stack of plates on the counter.

For a much more satisfying meal, direct the best chef in the house to Prepare a Meal. In this screen, Bella is getting ready to throw the raw ingredients into the food processor (a positive modifier, as noted in the table below). While one Sim prepares breakfast, you can assign the other Sims to menial labor, such as mopping or picking up garbage.

Thrilled that he doesn't have to eat his own tasteless slop, Mark grabs a plate from the counter.

Another option for preparing multiple portions is to call out for a pizza. This is a good choice for a Sim who has a low Cooking Skill. Rather than using the stove and setting the kitchen on fire, a telephone call and §40 will buy a hot pie, delivered to the door in an hour.

The Sims love their pizza, and they can't wait to set it down and grab a slice. So, don't be surprised if your Sim plops the carton down on the first available counter—even in the bathroom—and starts grazing.

How Appliances and Surfaces Affect Hunger Score

APPLIANCE/SURFACE	HUNGER POINTS ADDED TO MEAL
Dishwasher	5
Trash Compactor	5
Fridge (Llamark)	9
Toaster Oven	9 (plus Cooking Skill)
Fridge (Porcina)	12
Counter (Barcelona)	16
Counter (NuMica)	16
Counter (Tiled)	16
Fridge (Freeze Secret)	16
Microwave	16 (plus Cooking Skill)
Food Processor	32
Stove (Dialectric)	32 (plus 1.5 x Cooking Skill)
Stove (Pyrotorre)	48 (plus 1.5 x Cooking Skill)

CHAPTER 9:
SURVIVAL TIPS

Introduction

The beauty of playing *The Sims* is that everyone's experience is different. When you take a serious approach to shaping your family, the game can mirror your own life. However, if you mismanage your Sims, they can sink into despair, waving their little arms in the air over failed relationships, poor career decisions, or even a bad mattress. You can always delete your family and start over. But then you would never get that warm, fuzzy feeling that comes from turning your pitiful Sims' world into Shangri La.

This chapter is devoted to the *Sims* player who wants to go the distance and fight the good fight. Because most Sim problems can be traced back to one or more deficient Motive scores, we have arranged the following tips into separate Motive sections. Although some of the information is covered in other chapters, this is meant to be a quick-reference guide for times of crisis. Simply turn to the appropriate Motive and save your Sim's life with one of our game-tested tips.

Of course, you can also take a more devious approach to satisfying or altering your Sim's needs. Our Cheats section gives you a bundle of unofficial commands to rock your Sim's world. We take no responsibility for the results. (In other words, don't come crying to us if you stick your Sim in a room with no doors and he or she drops dead!).

Hunger

Maximize Food Quality and Preparation Time

For the best food quality, upgrade *all* appliances and countertops. Anything short of the most expensive refrigerator, countertop, stove, etc., reduces the potential Hunger value of your meals. Preparing a meal quickly is all about kitchen design. Align your objects in the order of preparation, beginning with the refrigerator, followed by the food processor (figure 9-1), and then ending with the stove (figure 9-2).

Fig. 9-1. The food goes from the refrigerator directly to the food processor.

Fig. 9-2. Next stop is the stove, right next door.

Have an open countertop next to the stove on the other side so the food preparer can set the plates down (figure 9-3). Although it has nothing to do with preparation, position the kitchen table and chairs close to the stove so that your Sims can grab their food, sit down together, and boost their Social scores (figure 9-4).

Fig. 9-5. After making dinner, our hard-working Sim can go to bed and sleep late in the morning.

Fig. 9-3. From the stove, the chef moves just a couple steps to the counter and sets down the plates.

Fig. 9-4. If your Sims are prompted to eat, they'll be ready to grab a plate as soon as it hits the counter, and with the table nearby, they can eat, chat, and make it to work on time.

Designate one Sim as your chef. Make sure that Sim has easy access to a chair and bookcase, and then set aside time each day to Study Cooking. When the resident chef's Cooking Skill reaches 10, you have achieved the pinnacle of food preparation.

After the food is on the counter, immediately send the Sim to bed. Most Sims should get up by 5, or the very latest, 6 a.m. to be on time for their morning jobs (the chef can sleep in). When everyone comes downstairs, breakfast (it's really dinner, but Sims don't care what you call it, as long as it doesn't have flies) will be on the counter (figure 9-6), fresh and ready to go. You'll save at least 20 Sim-minutes of morning prep time.

Fig. 9-6. It's only 5:30 a.m., but our Sim kid is already eating breakfast. After taking care of his Hygiene, he'll still have time for studying or boosting his Fun score before the school bus arrives.

Make Breakfast the Night Before

Sim food lasts for at least seven hours before the flies arrive and the food is officially inedible. If you have one Sim in the house who doesn't work, have him or her prepare breakfast for everyone at around midnight, as pictured in figure 9-5.

Comfort

When You Gotta Go, Go in Style

A toilet is often overlooked as a source of Comfort. The basic Hygeia-O-Matic Toilet costs only §300, but it provides zero Comfort. Spend the extra §900 and buy the Flush Force 5 XLT (figure 9-7). Your Sims have to use the bathroom anyway, so they might as well enjoy the +4 Comfort rating every time they take a seat.

Fig. 9-8. Our Sim is hungry, but he always has time to receive a nice Back Rub.

Fig. 9-7. You can live with a black-and-white TV for a while, but it doesn't make sense to do without the added comfort of the Flush Force.

Hygiene

Your Mother Was Right

One of the biggest contributors to declining Hygiene is the lack of hand washing after using the bathroom (in the Sims and in real life). If your Sim does not have a Neat personality, you may need to initiate this action. If you keep it up throughout the day, your Sim will be in better shape in the morning, when a shorter shower can be the difference between making the car pool or missing a day of work.

Rub Your Sim the Right Way

Giving another Sim a Back Rub is a great way to increase your chances of seeing Hug, and eventually Kiss on the social interaction menu. However, don't forget that it also raises the recipient's Comfort level. If your Sim's Comfort level is down, even after a long night's sleep, try a few Back Rubs. It will send your Sim to work in a better mood, which might be just enough to earn the next promotion.

Fig. 9-9. This Sim has an average Neat rating, which means she won't always wash her hands after using the bathroom. A few gentle reminders are in order.

Flush Your Troubles Away

Sad but true, sloppy Sims don't flush (figure 9-10). It's easy to overlook this nasty habit during a busy day, but it could lead to trouble. A clogged toilet may not affect Hygiene directly, but if your Sim is forced to pee on the floor because the toilet is not working, the Hygiene score drops dramatically.

Fig. 9-10. Second time tonight for this soldier, and we're still waiting for the first flush.

Bladder

Sorry, there's no magic formula for relieving a full Bladder. However, to guard against emergencies and the resulting puddles on the floor, try building two semi-private stalls in your bathroom. This allows two Sims to use the facilities without infringing on each other's privacy, as pictured in figure 9-11.

Fig. 9-11. Dual stalls improve the traffic flow (and other flows) in the bathroom.

Energy

Getting Enough Sleep with Baby

Nothing drains a Sim's Energy bar faster than having a baby in the house (figure 9-12). If you want to survive the three-day baby period without everyone losing their jobs, you must sleep when the baby sleeps. Most likely, this will be in the middle of the day, because Sim babies, like their real counterparts, couldn't care less about their parents' sleep schedules. The baby will not sleep for a full eight hours; however, if you get five or six hours of sleep with the baby, you'll have enough Energy to carry out other important household tasks.

Fig. 9-12. This Sim mom is at the end of her rope, and the baby is just getting warmed up.

Kids Make Great Babysitters

It does nothing for their Fun or Social levels, but Sim kids will dutifully care for their baby siblings. When they come home from school, feed them, allow a short play period, and then lock them in the room with the baby (if you're feeling particularly sadistic, you can go into Build mode and wall them in). They usually respond on their own, but you can always direct them to the crib, as pictured in figure 9-13, (unless they are too exhausted and need sleep). Take advantage of this time by sending the regular caregiver to bed for some much-needed sleep.

Fig. 9-13. Big brother makes a great nanny.

Favorite Fun Activities

TRAIT	BEST ACTIVITIES
Neat	N/A
Outgoing	TV (Romance), Hot Tub, Pool (if Playful is also high)
Active	Basketball, Stereo (dance), Pool, TV (Action)
Lazy	TV (as long as it's on, they're happy!), Computer, Book
Playful	Any fun object, including Computer, Dollhouse, Train Set, VR Glasses, Pinball, etc. If also Active, shift to Basketball, Dance, and Pool.
Serious	Chess, Newspaper, Book, Paintings (just let them stare)
Nice	Usually up for anything
Mean	TV (Horror)

Fun

Finding the Right Activity for Your Sim

Unless your Sims live in a monastery, you should have plenty of Fun objects in your house. The trick is matching the right kind of activity with a Sim's personality. In the frenzy of daily schedules and maintaining Relationships, it's easy to lose touch with your Sim's personality traits. Visit the Personality menu often (click on the "head" icon) to review the five traits. Make sure you have at least one of the following objects readily available to your Sim (the bedroom is a good spot).

When in Doubt, Entertain Someone

If your Sim does not have access to a Fun activity, simply Entertain someone for an instant Fun (and Social) boost, as pictured in figure 9-14. You can usually repeat this activity several times, and it doesn't take much time (great for kids on busy school mornings).

Fig. 9-14. When a good toy is not around, Sim kids love to Entertain each other.

> ## NOTE
>
> *A Sim should have at least six points (bars) in one of the following traits to maximize the recommended activity. Of course, an even higher number produces faster Fun rewards. To qualify for the opposite trait (e.g., Active/Lazy, Playful/Serious) a Sim should have no more than three points in the trait).*

Social

Satisfying Social requirements can be very frustrating, especially when Sims are on different work or sleep schedules. Socializing is a group effort, so plan small parties on a regular basis. Keep a notepad with all of your Sims' work schedules, so you know whom to invite at any time of the day.

- **It's O.K. to ask your guests to leave. After you shmooze a little and boost your Relationship score, send the Sim packing, and call up a different one. Use this round-robin approach to maintain all of your friendships.**

- **Don't let Mean Sims abuse you. This can be tough to control if you're not paying attention. When you're socializing with a Mean Sim, keep an eye on the activity queue in the screen's upper-left corner. If that Sim's head pops up (without you initiating it), it probably says "Be Teased by...," or "Be Insulted by...." Simply click on the icon to cancel the negative event and maintain your Relationship score. Once you diffuse the threat, engage the Sim in simple talking, or move your Sim into a group activity (pool table, hot tub, pool, etc.)**

- **Unless you like being the bad guy, don't advertise your advances toward one Sim if you already have a Relationship with another. Sims are extremely jealous, but you can still maintain multiple love relationships as long as you don't flaunt them in public.**

Room

A Room score crisis is easy to remedy. If you have the money, simply add more lights and paintings. Also check the quality of objects in the room, and upgrade whenever possible. If your room is jammed with expensive objects, lights, and paintings and your Room score is still low, there must be a mess somewhere. A normally maxed out Room score can slip with so much as a puddle on the floor (as pictured in figure 9-15). Clean up the mess to restore the Room score to its normal level.

Fig. 9-15. It looks like someone fell short of the toilet. A mop will take care of the mess and raise the Room score.

Scan your house on a regular basis for the following negative Room factors:

- **Dead plants**
- **Cheap objects (especially furniture)**
- **Puddles (they can also indicate a bad appliance; when in doubt, click on the item to see if Repair comes up as an option)**
- **Dark areas**
- **If you have the money, replace items taken by the Repo guy.**

Cheats

Activate the cheat command line at any time during a game by pressing Ctrl + Shift + C. An input box appears in the screen's upper left corner. Type in one of the codes listed below. You must re-activate the command line after each cheat is entered. The following cheats work only with Version 1.1 or later of *The Sims*.

Cheats

DESCRIPTION	CODE INPUT
1,000 Simoleans	rosebud
Import and load specific FAM file	import <FAM file>
Create moat or streams	water_tool
Create-a-character mode	edit_char
Display personality and interests	interests
Draw all animation disabled	draw_all_frames off
Draw all animation enabled	draw_all_frames on
Execute "file.cht" file as a list of cheats	cht <filename>
Floorable grid disabled	draw_floorable off
Floorable grid enabled	draw_floorable on
Map editor disabled	map_edit off
Map editor enabled	map_edit on
Move any object (on)	move_objects on
Move any object (off)	move_objects off
Preview animations disabled	preview_anims off
Preview animations enabled	preview_anims on
Quit game	quit
Rotate camera	rotation <0-3>
Save currently loaded house	save
Save family history file	history
Selected person's path displayed	draw_routes on

DESCRIPTION	CODE INPUT
Selected person's path hidden	draw_routes off
Set event logging mask	log_mask
Set free thinking level	autonomy <1-100>
Set game speed	sim_speed <-1000-1000>
Set grass change value	edit_grass <number>:
Set grass growth	grow_grass <0-150>
Set maximum milliseconds to allow simulator	sim_limit <milliseconds>
Set sim speed	sim_speed <-1000-1000>
Sets the neighborhood directory to the path	<directory path>
Start sim logging	sim_log begin
End sim logging	sim_log end
Swap the two house files and updates families	swap_houses <house number> <house number>
Ticks disabled	sweep off
Ticks enabled	sweep on
Tile information displayed	tile_info on
Tile information hidden	tile_info off
Toggle camera mode	cam_mode
Toggle music	music
Toggle sound log window	sound_log
Toggle sounds	sound
Toggle web page creation	html
Total reload of people skeletons, animations, suits, and skins	reload_people
Trigger sound event	soundevent

PART II:

The SiMs Vacation

EXPANSION PACK

CHAPTER 10: CABIN FEVER

Introduction

The *Vacation* expansion pack includes several dramatic improvements over the original *The Sims* game. The depth of each Sim's personality has expanded dramatically, with the addition of interest management, daily and lifetime relationship scores, and an incredible diversity of new interactions. The expanded interaction trees first introduced in *Hot Date* give *Vacation* a new level of nuance and Sim-strategy. *Vacation* goes even further by expanding all the children's interactions to the same level, completing the evolution of the Sims' social interaction system. This chapter helps you master all the game's new features.

Relationships

Sims now express their feelings for each other with a daily score and a lifetime score, instead of the all-inclusive relationship score. The daily score measures how a Sim feels about another Sim in the moment, and all interactions modify the daily score. The lifetime score, on the other hand, is the overall, lasting impression one Sim leaves on another.

Fig. 10-1. Sims veterans will immediately notice the twin relationship bars. The top bar is the daily relationship score, while the bottom is the lifetime relationship score.

NOTE

If you don't have the Hot Date *expansion installed, your existing Sims' relationships will translate into the new* Vacation *relationship scores when you install the expansion. Their new lifetime and daily scores will both be equal to their old score, making the transition seamless.*

Daily and Lifetime Relationships

In *The Sims*, Sims had only one relationship score. They liked each other all the time, were indifferent all the time, or hated each other all the time, depending on their relationship score. While this system was easy to manage, it meant that you could never have arguments with your friends, because they would cease to be your friends. In contrast, now you can have a spat with your spouse, a quarrel with your best friend, or even a good day with a Sim you just can't stand most of the time.

Fig. 10-2. Family feuds are now possible—your Sims can have a bad day without ending a relationship.

All interactions now have two facets, with an effect on the daily relationship score and a possible effect on the lifetime score. The daily score is roughly equivalent to the original *The Sims* relationship score, so look for the familiar interaction results in Sims' daily relationship scores. Very important or meaningful interactions also have an immediate effect on the lifetime score, though this will usually be only one or two points.

Fig. 10-3. Monumental interactions like passionate kisses or knock-down-drag-out fights immediately affect the lifetime relationship scores between two Sims.

Since only a few interactions directly affect them, lifetime relationships are much more sturdy than daily relationships, which change with each and every interaction. Daily relationships also decay with neglect, just as they did in *The Sims*. A lifetime relationship score, on the other hand, has no arbitrary decay. Instead, it slowly migrates toward the daily score through a fairly straightforward process.

Fig. 10-4. Since the lifetime relationship score isn't immediately changed by most daily interactions, you can see a significant difference between the two relationship scores in some cases.

Every half hour of Sim time, the lifetime relationship score moves toward the daily score by one point. If the daily score is higher than the lifetime score, lifetime goes up. If the daily score is lower, the lifetime score drops. The lifetime score continues to migrate toward the daily score until the two are equal. If you've had a spat with a friend, it's important to make amends quickly, or your lifetime score will suffer while you are apart. Conversely, it's harder to get really high lifetime scores, as they require constant positive interactions.

Interaction success is based on the daily relationship score of the Sims, not the lifetime score. While you have probably experienced an occasional failed interaction amongst your Sim families or friends due to mood, now you must be even more conscious of your Sims' current feelings. The daily relationship score overrides the lifetime relationship score, so you can't always count on successful interactions between close friends.

A long vacation can hurt your relationships with Sims you haven't seen in a long time. Sending postcards can alleviate this decay a little. See page 167 for more on postcards.

Kids Are People, Too

Vacation brings children's interactions to the same level as the new adult interactions first introduced in *Hot Date*. There are three main categories: child to child, adult to child, and child to adult. From hugging to horseplay, all your social interactions with children will now be much more fulfilling.

Fig. 10-5. Maggie takes advantage of her newfound ability to do a crazy dance.

New Interactions

Vacation includes entirely new categories of interactions, which not only increase the number of ways your Sims interact, but also dynamically expand *how* they interact. You now have greater control over how your Sims behave, and more importantly, you gain a great deal of information about the Sims with which you interact. Use this information to increase the success of your interactions by tailoring your actions to the other Sim's personality and mood.

Fig. 10-6. Existing interactions have been expanded with new submenus for a wide range of specific interactions.

In addition to the new interactions categories, almost all existing interactions have been expanded. Now you can choose exactly how to engage in a general interaction. Gone are the days when a kiss was just a kiss! Now, you can kiss on the hand, smack on the cheek, peck at the lips, or plunge into a steamy embrace that would make a sailor blush! Each specific interaction has its own criteria for acceptance or rejection, so tailoring your actions for maximum success is important.

Been There, Done That

In *The Sims*, you could build friendships with a simple formula of repetitive interactions: talk, talk, talk, compliment, talk, compliment, etc. Now, Sims pay attention to what you've been doing and will no longer accept repetitive cycles. In every 80-minute period of Sim time, a Sim only responds fully to a given interaction once. The second time it is initiated, the Sim remains indifferent, and no change occurs to either relationship score. If you attempt to use the same interaction a third time in any 80-minute period, the subject Sim rejects the interaction, resulting in a hit to your relationship scores.

NOTE

The only exception to the "three strikes" rule is talking interactions, which may be carried on indefinitely without direct penalty.

A new thought bubble icon represents a Sim's annoyance with repetition. Three drama faces followed by ellipses pop up over a Sim who is getting bored with a one-trick pony show. If your interactions lead to the display of the three strikes icon, change tactics. It's more important, however, to try to avoid this situation in the first place, since the display of the icon means the relationship damage has already been done.

Fig. 10-7. Even children get tired of doing the same thing over and over in *The Sims*.

Choosing Interactions

The new interactions can seem daunting, with dozens of choices for socialization at every meeting. The following descriptions and strategies will help you choose the right interaction with each Sim in your life. Following the interaction strategies is a set of tables listing all of the new interactions, their criteria for success or failure, and their possible outcomes.

The Ask Menu

The new Ask menu is one of your most powerful tools in relationship building. Its submenu gives you all of the questions you need to find out exactly what a fellow Sim needs, wants, and likes. Use that knowledge to cater your Sim's actions to the other's liking, saving you from the embarrassment of tickling a serious Sim or talking politics to a party animal. Asking questions is accepted by all but the most upset Sim, and the interaction gives the same boost to relationships that talking does. When the other Sim responds, pay attention to the thought bubble. It reveals the answer to the question you asked, which you can then use to improve your relationship.

Fig. 10-8. Asking questions gives you valuable insight into another Sim's disposition.

Ask — About Interests

You can ask another Sim about his or her interests by selecting Ask—About Interests. The response includes a few thought bubbles displaying the icons of three favorite interests. This is an important exposition, so take notes if you're serious about forming a relationship with that Sim. Match the interest icons with those shown in the "Self-Actualization: Interests" section later in this chapter, and then talk to the other Sim. Once engaged in conversation, select Talk—Change Subject. Select one of the interests that the Sim described, and select a common interest, or at least one that the other Sim mentioned. Talking about topics that interest both Sims results in the greatest relationship bonus.

Ask — About Needs

Asking about another Sim's needs is a good way to go about improving his or her mood. A good mood is essential for successful interactions, so it behooves you to take care of a guest's needs. The response indicates the Sim's lowest motive score at the time. This is completely relative, so you won't know if the Sim is at –50 across the board and happens to be –51 in hunger, or is at 95 in all scores save a 90 in bladder. Use overall behavior as a general mood indicator. If there's no spontaneous complaining, you probably have a basically happy Sim, and taking care of the most urgent need will boost overall mood. It is more difficult to take care of your guest's needs at home than a date's needs on vacation.

Fig. 10-9. Dianne says she's hungry, which helps us figure out what we should do next to keep our guest happy.

Assault and Battery

Shoving, slapping, and fighting hurt a relationship any way you look at it, but very playful Sims who are in a good mood may actually get a giggle out of a "sissy fight." This playful interaction is risky; a rejected attempt has the same result as an intentional slapping. If accepted, however, a sissy fight boosts the fun and social motives, plus the relationship. Because of the consequences of failure, be sure you know your subject is playful and in a good mood before trying this.

Fig. 10-11. Getting slapped by your audience is a sure sign that your joke failed.

Fig. 10-10. A sissy fight can be a fun diversion for a couple of playful Sims.

Teasing and Tickling

These two interaction categories are related, as they rely on the same kinds of factors for success or failure. Playful Sims who are in a good mood will enjoy these interactions, while those who are not will have varying negative reactions. If a Sim is both unhappy and serious, sparks will definitely fly when someone is silly enough to try these interactions. Therefore, save these types of interactions for Sims you know are playful, and make sure they are in a good mood by trying some other interactions first.

Flirtations

Flirtation carries with it the potential for some immediate improvement to both Sims' social motives, as well as a bump to both the daily and lifetime relationships. Flirtation is almost a sure-fire bet when a Sim has an established crush or love relationship with your Sim, but it can be risky between friends.

Greetings and Good-byes

You can now select the method your Sims use to mark the occasions of coming together and parting company. These interactions are special, because your window of success is limited both on the high end and low end of the scale. With most interactions, success occurs so long as a relationship is as good or better than a specific set of criteria. With greetings and good-byes, Sims also consider a maximum score of acceptance. In other words, if you simply wave good-bye to those who love you dearly instead of giving them a warm parting hug, you may hurt their feelings. Therefore, it's important to match your choices very carefully with your Sim's relationships.

Fig. 10-12. Even saying good-bye demands a little consideration with the new interactions.

Hugs and Kisses

With no less than 10 kinds of hugs and kisses (and that's just standing up!), you now have a multitude of ways to show that special Sim you care. Kisses do not have to be romantic anymore: pecks on the cheek, polite kisses, and kisses on the hand can all be shared between friends. On the other hand, a dip kiss will only be accepted by an established love interest, making it impossible to use as a love-inspiring romantic encounter.

> **TIP** The tame kisses have relatively low requirements for acceptance, so by all means, let the love flow!

Children's Interactions

The newly expanded pie menus give children the same depth and scope that adult Sims have enjoyed since the release of *Hot Date*. The following strategies are for the exclusive interactions involving children. Children also have some of the same interactions as adults. For those interactions, use the strategies in the previous section, but note it is always easier to get a successful interaction with a child than between two adults.

Annoying Habits

Children annoy each other with varying degrees of severity, from poking all the way up to kicking. Naturally, the interaction is detrimental to the relationship, although the bully can enjoy up to 10 points of gain in social motive if the victim gets upset. This interaction is not beneficial to the relationship for either party, so it's really best used as an amusement, or to form a truly monumental hatred between young Sims.

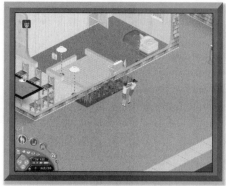

Fig. 10-13. Nothing like a swift kick in the shin to get a play session off on the wrong foot!

Bragging Rights

Kids can lay it on almost as well as adults, and the new brag interaction lets them talk about themselves until they are blue in the face. Fortunately for young and vain Sims, children have a higher tolerance for such things than adults do, so as long as the relationship is at least fair, a bragging session will be well received. Use it like a compliment in adult interactions: get to relationship 10, and a mood of ≤ 20, then bring out the self-promotion.

Cheer Up

Children can lift the moods of their parents and peers with a little pep talk. This option only appears when the child is in a good mood and the subject is in a bad mood. As long as the subject likes the child, it will be accepted, making it far more effective than adult cheering.

Entertainment

Children can entertain and be entertained by both children and adults, and as with most child interactions, it's much easier to get a successful result. Use it early in a play session, as it is entirely mood based—the subject doesn't even have to like the entertainer, as long as one party in the interaction is a child. Successful entertainment interactions carry a large motive and relationship bonus, so use this interaction liberally.

Fig. 10-14. All children enjoy being entertained—even by people they don't like.

Playground Games

Playing tag is the same old favorite from *The Sims*. Rock-paper-scissors is new, and it requires a good relationship and a good mood. Adults can also roughhouse with children, which results in a large social motive and relationship increase. Playing is generally accepted so long as the subject is in a fairly good mood.

Scolding

This adult-to-child interaction is hard to pull off successfully, but carries little penalty if rejected. The child must be in a very bad mood: worse than –10. Essentially this is the second red bar on the mood indicator, which you can check by clicking on the child.

If the interaction is successful, the child will respond very positively, with a strong increase in social motive and lifetime relationship.

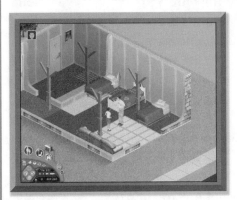

Fig. 10-15. Scolding can actually be a relationship builder in Sim families.

Interaction Tables

The following tables contain all relevant data for every interaction in *The Sims*. The interactions are broken down into four sections: adult to adult, adult to child, child to adult, and child to child. Each section contains three tables. The first table describes the general requirements (some of which are lengthy) for a successful interaction, and the second lists the effects of all possible results of each interaction. The third lists the conditions that determine whether or not a specific interaction shows up as an option in your pie menus. Use these tables to gauge your chance of success with each interaction. Combined with the new Ask interactions, these tables can help you potentially reduce your failed interactions to near zero!

Adult-to-Adult Interactions

Key	
>	Greater than
≥	Greater than or equal to
<	Less than
≤	Less than or equal to

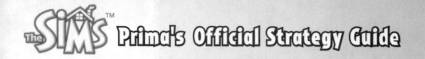

Adult Interaction Success Requirements

CATEGORY	INTERACTION	INITIATOR REQUIREMENTS	RECIPIENT REQUIREMENTS
Ask	How Are You?	None	Mood ≥ -80
	How's Work?	None	Mood ≥ -30
	Invite Downtown	None	Energy ≥ 0, Daily ≥ -20
	Invite Home	None	Mood ≥ 40, Outgoing > 9
		None	Mood ≥ 40, Lifetime > 50
		None	Mood ≥ 40, Daily ≥ 55, Outgoing > 5
		None	Mood ≥ 40, Daily ≥ 70
	Let's Hang Out/Date	Hygiene > -10	Daily > 10
	Move In	None	Lifetime ≥ 60, Mood ≥ 45, Daily ≥ 85
	Propose	Different Genders	Love, Lifetime > 80, Daily > 75, Mood > 60
	What Are You Into?	None	Mood ≥ -30
Attack	Fight	Body ≥ Recipient's Body	None
	Shove	Body ≥ Recipient's Body +2	None
	Slap	Body > Recipient's Body	None
	Slap Fight	None	Daily ≥ 20, Mood ≥ 10, Playful ≥ 6
Brag	Boast	None	Daily between 0 and 25, Mood > 10
	Flex	None	Nice ≥ 9
		Body > Recipient's Body +5	None
		None	Daily ≥ 30
		None	Mood ≥ 25
	Primp	None	Daily ≥ 50
		None	Daily > 0, Outgoing > 6
		None	Daily > 0, Mood ≥ 35
Cheer Up	Comfort	None	Daily ≥ 65
		None	Daily > 55, Outgoing ≤ 3
	Encourage	None	Outgoing > 7
		None	Mood ≥ -25
	With Puppet	None	Playful > 7
		None	Nice ≥ 4, Mood ≥ -30
		None	Nice < 4, Mood ≥ -40

Adult Interaction Success Requirements, continued

CATEGORY	INTERACTION	INITIATOR REQUIREMENTS	RECIPIENT REQUIREMENTS
Compliment	Admire	None	Nice ≤ 3, Mood > 60
		None	Nice > 3, Daily > -25
		None	Nice > 3, Mood > 10
	Worship	None	Daily ≥ 20, Charisma ≥ 7
		None	Daily ≥ 20, Outgoing ≤ 3, Mood > 60
		None	Daily ≥ 20, Outgoing > 3, Nice > 4
		None	Daily ≥ 20, Outgoing > 3, Nice ≤ 3, Mood > 60
Dance	Lively	None	Daily > -10, Energy ≥ 10, Mood ≥ 0, Outgoing > 3
		None	Daily > -10, Energy ≥ 10, Mood ≥ 0, Outgoing ≤ 3, Mood > 40
		None	Daily > -10, Energy ≥ 10, Mood ≥ 0, Outgoing ≤ 3, Daily > 30
	Slow	Hygiene > 20	Energy > 10, Mood > 20, Daily > -10, Outgoing > 3
		Hygiene > 20	Energy > 10, Mood > 20, Daily > -10, Lifetime ≥ 35
		Hygiene > 20	Energy > 10, Mood > 40, Outgoing ≤ 3
		Hygiene > 20	Energy > 10, Mood > 20, Daily > 30, Lifetime ≥ 35
Entertain	Joke	None	Playful > 7
		None	Playful < 3, Daily > 30
		None	Playful ≥ 3, Mood > 50, Daily > 30
	(Mild Accept)	None	Playful ≥ 3, Daily < -10
	(Mild Accept)	None	Playful < 3, Mood > 50, Daily < -10
	Juggle	None	Playful > 7
		None	Playful ≥ 3, Daily > 20
		None	Playful < 3, Mood > 50, Daily > 20
	With Puppet	None	Nice < 4, Mood > 50
		None	Nice ≥ 3, Playful ≥ 7
		None	Nice ≥ 3, Playful < 3, Mood > 50

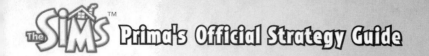

Adult Interaction Success Requirements, continued

CATEGORY	INTERACTION	INITIATOR REQUIREMENTS	RECIPIENT REQUIREMENTS
Flirt	Check Out	None	Mood ≥ -10, Outgoing ≥ 7
		None	Mood ≥ -10, Outgoing > 2, Mood > 40
		None	Mood ≥ -10, Outgoing > 2, Daily > 20
		None	Mood ≥ -10, Outgoing ≤ 2, Charisma ≥ 3
		None	Mood ≥ -10, Outgoing ≤ 2, Body ≥ 5
		None	Mood ≥ -10, Outgoing ≤ 2, Mood > 30
		None	Mood ≥ -10, Outgoing ≤ 2, Daily > 15
	Growl	None	Mood ≥ 20, Outgoing ≥ 9
		None	Mood < 20, Lifetime ≥ 30
		None	Outgoing ≥ 4
		None	Mood > 50
		None	Daily > 25
	Back Rub	None	Mood > 20, Daily or Lifetime > 35
		None	Mood > 20, Outgoing ≥ 6
		None	Mood > 20, Daily > 30
	Sweet Talk	None	Daily or Lifetime ≥ 40
Greet	Wave	None	Lifetime > -40
	Shake Hands	None	Lifetime ≥ -20
	Air Kiss	None	Lifetime ≥ 20
	Kiss Cheek	None	Lifetime ≥ 20
	Hug	None	Lifetime > -20
	Romantic Kiss	None	Lifetime ≥ 50
		In Love	In Love
	Suave Kiss	None	Lifetime > 15
Hug	Friendly	Hygiene ≥ -40	Mood > 50
		Hygiene ≥ -40	Daily > 30
		Hygiene ≥ -40	Nice ≥ 2, Mood > 10
	Intimate	Hygiene ≥ -40	Nice ≥ 3, Daily > 20
		Hygiene ≥ -40	Nice < 3, Mood > 60
		Hygiene ≥ -40	Nice < 3, Daily or Lifetime > 30

Adult Interaction Success Requirements, continued

CATEGORY	INTERACTION	INITIATOR REQUIREMENTS	RECIPIENT REQUIREMENTS
	Leap into Arms	Hygiene ≥ -40	Nice or Playful ≥ 7
		Hygiene ≥ -40	Mood > 40
		Hygiene ≥ -40	Daily > 45
		Hygiene ≥ -40	Lifetime > 30
	Romantic	Hygiene ≥ -40	Nice < 3, Mood > 60
		Hygiene ≥ -40	Nice < 3, Daily > 50
		Hygiene ≥ -40	Nice < 3, Lifetime > 40
		Hygiene ≥ -40	Nice ≥ 3, Daily > 30
		Hygiene ≥ -40	Nice ≥ 3, Lifetime > 35
Insult	Shake Fist	None	Nice ≥ 4, -30 < Mood < 0
		None	Nice ≥ 4, Mood > 0, Daily ≤ 20
	Poke	None	Nice < 4
		None	Nice ≥ 4, Mood ≤ 0
		None	Nice ≥ 4, Mood > 0, Daily < 20
Kiss	Peck	None	Mood > 0, Lifetime ≥ 10, Daily ≥ 20
		None	Mood > 0, Daily ≥ 20
	Polite	None	Daily ≥ 20, Lifetime > 10, Mood ≥ 25
	Suave	None	Mood > 0, Lifetime ≥ 15, Daily ≥ 30
	Romantic	None	Crush
		None	Daily > 60, Mood > 40
		None	Lifetime > 60
	Passionate	None	Lifetime > 40, Daily ≥ 50, Mood ≥ 30
	Deep Kiss	None	Love, Mood ≥ 40
Nag	About Friends	None	Mood > 40
		None	Mood ≥ 0, Nice ≥ 7
	About House	None	Mood > 40
		None	Mood ≥ 0, Nice ≥ 7
	About Money	None	Mood > 40
		None	Mood ≥ 0, Nice ≥ 7
Plead	Apologize	None	Mood > -5
		None	Lifetime ≥ 25
	Grovel	None	Mood ≥ -15
		None	Lifetime ≥ 25

Adult Interaction Success Requirements, continued

CATEGORY	INTERACTION	INITIATOR REQUIREMENTS	RECIPIENT REQUIREMENTS
Say Good-bye	Shoo	None	Daily ≤ 10
	Shake Hands	None	Daily ≥ 20
		None	Lifetime ≥ 10
	Wave	None	Daily or Lifetime ≤ 20
	Kiss Cheek	None	Daily ≥ 20
		None	Lifetime ≥ 30
	Hug	None	Daily or Lifetime ≥ 30
	Kiss Hand	None	Nice ≤ 3, Daily ≥ 60
		None	Nice ≤ 3, Lifetime ≥ 50
		None	Nice > 3, Daily or Lifetime ≥ 40
	Polite Kiss	None	Outgoing ≥ 6, Daily ≥ 40
		None	Outgoing ≥ 6, Lifetime ≥ 60
		None	Outgoing < 6, Daily or Lifetime ≥ 60
	Passionate Kiss	None	Outgoing ≥ 7, Daily ≥ 60
		None	Outgoing ≥ 7, Lifetime ≥ 65
		None	Outgoing < 7, Daily ≥ 80
		None	Outgoing < 7, Lifetime ≥ 65
Talk	About Interests	(Always Accepted)	None
	Change Subject	(Always Accepted)	None
	Gossip	None	Daily > 40
Tease	Imitate	None	Playful > 6, Mood > 50
		None	Playful > 6, Mood < 0
		None	Daily ≥ -15, Lifetime > 50, Playful ≤ 6
	Taunt	None	Mood or Daily > -20
	Raspberry	None	Mood or Daily ≥ -20, Lifetime > 25
	Scare	None	Playful ≥ 5
		None	Mood > 25
Tickle	Ribs	None	Playful > 5
		None	Mood > 50
	Extreme	None	Playful > 5
		None	Mood > 50

Adult Social Interaction Results

INTERACTION	RESPONSE	DAILY RELATIONSHIP CHANGE	LIFETIME RELATIONSHIP CHANGE	SOCIAL SCORE CHANGE
ATTACKS				
Slap	Cry	0	0	3
	Slap Back	-10	-3	-7
Be Slapped	Cry	-20	-10	-17
	Slap Back	-15	-7	3
Sissy Fight	Cry	0	0	3
	Fight Back	-8	-2	-5
Be Sissy Fought	Cry	-16	-8	-13
	Fight Back	-13	-5	3
Shove	Cry	0	0	3
	Shove Back	-8	-2	-5
Be Shoved	Cry	-16	-8	-13
	Shove Back	-13	-5	3
BRAGGING				
Brag	Good	5	0	10
	Bad	-5	0	0
Be Bragged To	Good	3	0	5
	Bad	-5	0	0
INSULTS				
Insult	Cry	-6	-3	0
	Stoic	0	-1	3
	Angry	-10	-1	5
Be Insulted	Cry	-12	-5	-10
	Stoic	-8	0	-5
	Angry	-14	-2	-7
TEASING				
Taunt	Giggle	4	0	7
	Cry	0	0	3
Be Taunted	Giggle	4	0	7
	Cry	-10	0	-7

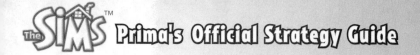

Adult Social Interaction Results, continued

INTERACTION	RESPONSE	DAILY RELATIONSHIP CHANGE	LIFETIME RELATIONSHIP CHANGE	SOCIAL SCORE CHANGE
Imitate with Puppet	Giggle	4	0	7
	Cry	0	0	3
Be Imitated with Puppet	Giggle	4	0	7
	Cry	-10	0	-7
Scare	Laugh	5	0	10
	Angry	-5	0	0
Be Scared	Laugh	5	0	8
	Angry	-10	0	0
TICKLING				
Tickle	Laugh	8	0	10
	Refuse	-5	-1	0
Be Tickled	Laugh	5	0	10
	Refuse	-8	-2	0
Extreme Tickle	Laugh	8	0	10
	Refuse	-5	-1	0
Be Extreme Tickled	Laugh	5	0	10
	Refuse	-5	-1	0
CHEERING				
Motivate	Good	5	0	7
	Mild	0	0	5
	Bad	-3	0	0
Be Motivated	Good	10	0	10
	Mild	0	0	5
	Bad	-10	0	0
Cheer Up with Puppet	Good	5	0	7 (Sensitive: 6)
	Mild	0	0	5
	Bad	-3	0	0
Be Cheered Up with Puppet	Good	6	0	10
	Mild	0	0	5
	Bad	-10	0	0

Adult Social Interaction Results, continued

INTERACTION	RESPONSE	DAILY RELATIONSHIP CHANGE	LIFETIME RELATIONSHIP CHANGE	SOCIAL SCORE CHANGE
COMPLIMENTS				
Admire	Accept	4	1	5
	Reject	-10	-1	0
Be Admired	Accept	3	2	11
	Reject	-7	-2	0
Worship	Accept	3	1	5
	Reject	-15	-5	0
Be Worshiped	Accept	4	2	15
	Reject	-10	-4	0
DANCING				
Dance Lively	Accept	6	0	13
	Reject	-5	0	0
Be Danced with Lively	Accept	6	0	13
	Reject	-5	0	0
Dance Slow	Accept	8	2	15
	Reject	-10	-3	-4
Be Danced with Slowly	Accept	8	2	15
	Reject	-7	-2	0
ENTERTAINING				
Joke	Laugh	3	0	9
	Giggle	2	0	7
	Fail	-6	0	0
Hear Joke	Laugh	4	0	10
	Giggle	3	0	7
	Fail	-7	0	0
Juggle or Puppet	Laugh	3	0	7
	Fail	-10	0	0
Watch Juggle	Laugh	4	0	10
	Fail	-7	0	0
Watch Puppet	Laugh	4	0	13
	Fail	-7	0	0

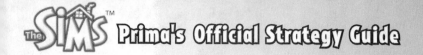

Adult Social Interaction Results, continued

INTERACTION	RESPONSE	DAILY RELATIONSHIP CHANGE	LIFETIME RELATIONSHIP CHANGE	SOCIAL SCORE CHANGE
FLIRTATION				
Give Backrub	Accept	3	2	7
	Reject	-7	-2	0
Receive Backrub	Accept	5	3	10
	Reject	-10	-3	0
Give Suggestion	Accept	4	1	10
	Ignore	-5	0	0
	Reject	-5	-1	-10
Receive Suggestion	Accept	6	1	10
	Ignore	-3	0	0
	Reject	-7	-2	0
Check Out	Accept	5	2	10
	Ignore	-5	0	0
	Reject	-8	-1	-10
Be Checked Out	Accept	5	2	10
	Ignore	-3	0	0
	Reject	-10	-3	0
Growl	Accept	5	2	10
	Ignore	-5	0	0
	Reject	-8	-2	-10
Receive Growl	Accept	6	2	10
	Ignore	-3	0	0
	Reject	-10	-3	0
GOOD-BYES				
Shake Hand	Good	2	0	0
	Bad	-2	0	0
Have Hand Shaken	Good	2	0	0
	Bad	-2	0	0
Hug	Good	5	0	0
	Bad	-5	0	0
Be Hugged	Good	5	0	0
	Bad	-5	0	0

Adult Social Interaction Results, continued

INTERACTION	RESPONSE	DAILY RELATIONSHIP CHANGE	LIFETIME RELATIONSHIP CHANGE	SOCIAL SCORE CHANGE
Polite Kiss	Good	7	2	0
	Bad	-7	-3	0
Be Politely Kissed	Good	7	3	0
	Bad	-7	-2	0
Kiss Cheek	Good	3	0	0
	Bad	-3	0	0
Have Cheek Kissed	Good	3	0	0
	Bad	-3	0	0
Kiss Hand	Good	3	1	0
	Bad	-3	-3	0
Have Hand Kissed	Good	3	2	0
	Bad	-3	-2	0
Passionate Kiss	Good	10	5	0
	Bad	-10	-6	0
Be Passionately Kissed	Good	10	5	0
	Bad	-10	-6	0
Wave	Good	1	0	0
	Bad	-1	0	0
Be Waved To	Good	1	0	0
	Bad	-1	0	0
Shoo	Good	1	0	0
	Neutral	0	0	0
	Bad	0	0	0
Be Shooed	Good	1	0	0
	Neutral	0	0	0
	Bad	-3	0	0

GREETINGS

INTERACTION	RESPONSE	DAILY RELATIONSHIP CHANGE	LIFETIME RELATIONSHIP CHANGE	SOCIAL SCORE CHANGE
Wave	Good	1	0	2
	Bad	-2	0	2
Shake Hand	Good	1	0	2
	Bad	-2	-2	0

Adult Social Interaction Results, continued

INTERACTION	RESPONSE	DAILY RELATIONSHIP CHANGE	LIFETIME RELATIONSHIP CHANGE	SOCIAL SCORE CHANGE
Have Hand Shaken	Good	2	1	0
	Bad	-2	-2	0
Air Kiss	Good	2	0	3
	Bad	-4	0	-3
Be Air Kissed	Good	2	0	3
	Bad	-4	0	-3
Polite Kiss	Good	5	1	5
	Bad	-8	-2	-4
Be Politely Kissed	Good	5	5	1
	Bad	-6	-1	-3
Kiss Hand	Good	5	1	5
	Bad	-6	-2	-5
Have Hand Kissed	Good	5	1	10
	Bad	-6	-1	-3
Hug	Good	8	2	8
	Bad	-8	-2	-4
Be Hugged	Good	8	2	8
	Bad	-8	-1	-3
Romantic Kiss	Good	12	3	12
	Bad	-12	-2	-5
Be Romantically Kissed	Good	12	3	12
	Bad	-12	-2	-3

HUGS

INTERACTION	RESPONSE	DAILY RELATIONSHIP CHANGE	LIFETIME RELATIONSHIP CHANGE	SOCIAL SCORE CHANGE
Friendly Hug	Accept	4	1	8
	Tentative	2	0	5
	Refuse	-5	-1	0
Receive Friendly Hug	Accept	5	1	8
	Tentative	4	0	5
	Refuse	-5	-1	0
Body Hug	Accept	5	2	10
	Tentative	5	0	7
	Refuse	-10	-3	0

Adult Social Interaction Results, continued

INTERACTION	RESPONSE	DAILY RELATIONSHIP CHANGE	LIFETIME RELATIONSHIP CHANGE	SOCIAL SCORE CHANGE
Be Body Hugged	Accept	8	2	10
	Tentative	4	0	7
	Refuse	-10	-2	0
Romantic Hug	Accept	5	2	10
	Tentative	5	0	7
	Reject	-10	-3	0
Be Romantically Hugged	Accept	8	2	10
	Tentative	4	0	7
	Reject	-10	-2	0
Flying Hug	Accept	9	2	10
	Refuse	-15	-4	0
Receive Flying Hug	Accept	8	2	10
	Tentative	4	0	7
	Refuse	-10	-2	0

KISSES

INTERACTION	RESPONSE	DAILY RELATIONSHIP CHANGE	LIFETIME RELATIONSHIP CHANGE	SOCIAL SCORE CHANGE
Kiss Hand	Passionate	5	0	5
	Polite	4	0	4
	Deny	-5	-1	4
Have Hand Kissed	Passionate	5	0	5
	Polite	4	0	4
	Deny	-5	0	0
Kiss Polite	Passionate	6	1	7
	Polite	5	0	5
	Deny	-7	-1	4
Be Kissed Politely	Passionate	6	1	7
	Polite	5	0	5
	Deny	-6	-1	0
Kiss Tentatively	Passionate	8	2	8
	Polite	6	1	6
	Deny	-9	-2	4

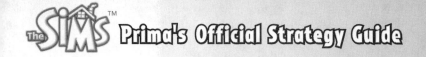

Adult Social Interaction Results, continued

INTERACTION	RESPONSE	DAILY RELATIONSHIP CHANGE	LIFETIME RELATIONSHIP CHANGE	SOCIAL SCORE CHANGE
Be Kissed Tentatively	Passionate	8	2	8
	Polite	6	1	6
	Deny	-8	-2	0
Kiss Passionately	Passionate	13	4	10
	Polite	8	2	8
	Deny	-10	-3	4
Be Kissed Passionately	Passionate	13	3	10
	Polite	8	2	8
	Deny	-10	-4	0
Dip Kiss	Passionate	15	5	15
	Polite	10	2	10
	Deny	-15	-5	4
Be Dip Kissed	Passionate	15	5	15
	Polite	10	2	10
	Deny	-15	-5	0
NAGGING				
Nag	Giggle	-1	0	3
	Cry	-4	-1	3
Be Nagged	Giggle	-3	0	4
	Cry	-8	-2	-5
PLEADING				
Apologize	Accept	8	0	8
	Reject	-8	0	3
Be Apologized To	Accept	8	0	8
	Reject	-5	0	3
Grovel	Accept	12	0	8
	Reject	-12	0	3
Be Groveled To	Accept	12	0	8
	Reject	-5	0	3

Adult Interaction Menu Triggers

CATEGORY	INTERACTION	RELATIONSHIP REQUIREMENTS	DISPOSITION REQUIREMENTS
Ask	How Are You?	Daily > -80	Mood > -70
	How's Work?	Daily between −5 and 35, Lifetime < 40	Mood > 0
	Invite Downtown	None	At Home Only
	Invite Home	Daily > 55	Downtown Only
	Let's Hang Out/Date	None	Always Available Downtown
	Move In	Lifetime > 50, Daily > 50	Same Gender
	Propose	Daily > 75	Different Genders, In Love
	What Are You Into?	Daily between −5 and 35, Lifetime < 40	Mood > 0
Attack	Fight	Daily < -40, Lifetime < 0	Mood < 0
	Shove	Lifetime ≤ 30, Daily < -40	Mood < 0
	Slap	Lifetime ≤ 30, Daily < -40	Mood < 0
	Slapfight	Daily < -40	Playful ≥ 7, Mood < 0
Brag	Boast	None	Daily < 50, Lifetime < 40
	Flex	Daily < 50, Lifetime < 40	Body ≥ 4
	Primp	Daily < 50, Lifetime < 40	Charisma ≥ 2
Cheer Up	Comfort	Lifetime > 25, Friends	Outgoing > 3, Mood > 25, Subject's Mood < 0
		Lifetime > 5, Friends	Outgoing ≤ 3, Mood > 20, Subject's Mood < 0
	Encourage	Lifetime > 25, Friends	Charisma ≥ 2, Mood > 25
	With Puppet	Friends	Playful ≥ 6, Outgoing ≥ 4, Mood > 25, Subject's Mood < 0
Compliment	Admire	Daily between -10 and 40	Mood > 20
	Worship	Daily between -10 and 40, Lifetime between 20 and 80,	Nice > 3, Outgoing > 3 Mood > 20
Dance	Lively	Daily > 30, Lifetime > -25	Energy > 20, Mood > -20, Outgoing > 3
	Slow	Lifetime > 20	Energy > 10

Adult Interaction Menu Triggers, continued

CATEGORY	INTERACTION	RELATIONSHIP REQUIREMENTS	DISPOSITION REQUIREMENTS
Entertain	Joke	Daily > 0, Lifetime between –25 and 70	Playful ≥3, Mood > -10
	Juggle	Daily > -25, Lifetime between 0 and 70	Outgoing > 3, Playful > 4 Mood > 0
	With Puppet	Daily > -25, Lifetime between 0 and 70	Outgoing > 3, Playful > 3 Mood > 0
Flirt	Check Out	Lifetime between –10 and 10, Daily between 5 and 60	Mood > -20
	Growl	Lifetime between –10 and 10, Daily between 5 and 60	Mood > -20
	Backrub	Daily between 30 and 60, Lifetime > 30	Mood > 30
	Sweet Talk	Daily between 25 and 60, Lifetime > -50	Outgoing ≥ 7, Mood > 30
		Daily between 40 and 60, Lifetime > -50	Outgoing < 7, Mood > 30
Greet	Wave	Always Available	
	Shake Hands	Always Available	
	Air Kiss	Lifetime ≥ 5	None
	Kiss Cheek	Lifetime ≥ 20	None
	Hug	Crush	None
	Romantic Kiss	Crush	None
	Suave Kiss	Lifetime > 15	Outgoing ≥ 3
Hug	Friendly	Lifetime > 0, Daily > 15	Mood > 10
	Intimate	Lifetime > 10, Daily > 15	Mood > 20
	Leap into Arms	Daily > 40, Lifetime > 30	Mood > 25, Outgoing > 5
	Romantic	Daily > 40, Lifetime > 40	Mood > 35, Outgoing > 3
Insult	Shake Fist	Lifetime < 50	Nice ≤ 3
		None	Mood < 0
	Poke	Lifetime < 50	Nice < 3
		None	Mood ≤ 0
Kiss	Peck	Daily ≥ 20, Lifetime > 0	Mood > 0
	Polite	Daily ≥ 35, Lifetime > 15	Mood > 15
	Suave	Daily ≥ 25, Lifetime > 10	Mood > 0
	Romantic	Daily ≥ 55, Lifetime > 25	Mood > 25
	Passionate	Daily ≥ 45, Lifetime > 25	Mood > 15
	Deep Kiss	Love	Mood > 25

Adult Interaction Menu Triggers, continued

CATEGORY	INTERACTION	RELATIONSHIP REQUIREMENTS	DISPOSITION REQUIREMENTS
Nag	About Friends	Lifetime > 40	Mood ≤ -30
	About House	Lifetime > 40	Mood ≤ -30
	About Money	Lifetime > 40	Mood ≤ -3, Cash < §1,000
Plead	Apologize	Daily ≤ -10 Lifetime > 5	Mood ≤ -20
	Grovel	Daily > -20, Lifetime > 10	Mood ≤ -40
Say Good-bye	Shoo	Daily < -50	None
	Shake Hands	Daily > -50	None
	Wave	Daily > -50	None
	Kiss Cheek	Daily > -10	None
	Hug	Daily > 0	None
	Kiss Hand	Daily > 20	None
	Polite Kiss	Daily ≥ 20	None
	Passionate Kiss	Daily > 20	Outgoing ≥ 7
		Daily > 40	Outgoing < 7
Talk	About Interests	None	Available in Ongoing Conversation
	Change Subject	None	Available in Ongoing Conversation
	Gossip	None	Mood > -25
Tease	Imitate	None	Playful > 5, Mood < 15
		Daily < -20	Playful > 5, Nice < 5
	Taunt	None	Mood < 30, Nice < 5
		Daily < -20	Nice < 5
	Raspberry	None	Mood < 15, Nice < 5
		Daily < -20	Nice < 5
	Scare	None	Playful ≥ 5, Mood < 30, Nice < 5
Tickle	Ribs	Daily > 10	Playful ≥4, Nice > 4
	Extreme	Daily > 10, Lifetime between 20 and 70	Playful > 3, Nice > 4

Adult-to-Child Interactions

Adult-to-Child Interaction Success Requirements

CATEGORY	INTERACTION	RECIPIENT REQUIREMENTS
Brag		Mood > 50, Daily > 50
Cheer Up		Social ≤ 0
		Daily ≥ 0
Entertain	Joke	Playful ≥ 2
		Mood ≥ 30
	Juggle	Playful ≥ 2
		Mood ≥ 30
Hug	Nice	Mood ≥ 20
		Daily ≥ 10
	Friendly	Mood ≥ 20
		Daily ≥ 10
Insult		Daily ≥ 25
Play	Rough House	Mood ≥ 20
Scold		Mood ≥ -25
Tease	Scare	Mood between -10 and 15
	Taunt	Daily ≥ 10
Tickle		Mood ≥ 15, Playful ≥ 1

Adult-to-Child Interaction Results

INTERACTION	RESPONSE	DAILY RELATIONSHIP CHANGE	LIFETIME RELATIONSHIP CHANGE	SOCIAL SCORE CHANGE
Brag	Accept	5	0	10
	Reject	-5	-1	0
Be Bragged To	Accept	3	0	5
	Reject	-5	-1	0
Cheer Up	Accept	5	0	7
	Reject	-3	0	0
Be Cheered Up	Accept	10	2	7
	Reject	-10	-2	0

Adult-to-Child Interaction Results, continued

INTERACTION	RESPONSE	DAILY RELATIONSHIP CHANGE	LIFETIME RELATIONSHIP CHANGE	SOCIAL SCORE CHANGE
Entertain—Joke	Accept	3	1	9
	Reject	-6	0	0
Be Entertained—Joke	Accept	4	2	10
	Reject	-7	0	0
Entertain—Juggle	Accept	3	1	7
	Reject	-10	-2	0
Be Entertained—Juggle	Accept	4	2	10
	Reject	-7	-1	0
Hug—Nice	Accept	4	1	8
	Reject	-5	-1	0
Be Hugged—Nice	Accept	4	1	8
	Reject	-5	-1	0
Hug—Friendly	Accept	5	2	10
	Reject	-10	-3	0
Be Hugged—Friendly	Accept	5	2	10
	Reject	-10	-2	-2
Insult	Accept	-10	-1	5
	Reject	-6	-3	0
Be Insulted	Accept	-14	-3	-7
	Reject	-12	-5	-10
Play—Rough House	Accept	3	1	9
	Reject	-6	0	0
Be Played With—Rough House	Accept	4	2	10
	Reject	-7	0	0
Scold	Accept	5	3	5
	Reject	-8	-3	2
Be Scolded	Accept	5	3	10
	Reject	-10	-2	-2

Adult-to-Child Interaction Results, continued

INTERACTION	RESPONSE	DAILY RELATIONSHIP CHANGE	LIFETIME RELATIONSHIP CHANGE	SOCIAL SCORE CHANGE
Tease—Scare	Accept	5	1	10
	Reject	-5	-1	0
Be Teased—Scare	Accept	5	1	8
	Reject	-10	-2	0
Tease—Taunt	Accept	4	0	7
	Reject	-3	0	-3
Be Teased—Taunt	Accept	4	1	7
	Reject	-10	-1	-7
Tickle	Accept	8	1	10
	Reject	-5	-1	0
Be Tickled	Accept	5	1	10
	Reject	-8	-2	0

Adult-to-Child Interaction Menu Triggers

CATEGORY	INTERACTION	INITIATOR REQUIREMENTS	RECIPIENT REQUIREMENTS
Brag		Mood < 10, Daily ≥ 10, Daily ≤ 50	None
Cheer Up		Mood ≥ 25, Daily ≥ 25	Mood ≤ 0
Entertain	Joke	Playful ≥ 4, Mood ≥ 40	None
		Mood > 50	None
	Juggle	Playful ≥ 5, Mood ≥ 40	None
		Mood ≥ 50	None
Hug	Nice	Daily ≥ 30, Mood > 30	None
	Friendly	Daily ≥ 35, Mood > 35	None
Insult		Mood ≤ -10	None
Play	Rough House	Playful ≥ 4, Mood ≥ 20	None
		Mood ≥ 40	None
Scold		None	Mood ≤ -10

Adult-to-Child Interaction Menu Triggers, continued

CATEGORY	INTERACTION	INITIATOR REQUIREMENTS	RECIPIENT REQUIREMENTS
Tease	Scare	Mood ≤ 5	None
		Daily ≤ -5	None
	Taunt	Mood ≤ 15	None
		Daily ≤ -5	None
Tickle		Playful ≥ 2, Mood ≥ 0	None
		Mood > 30	None

Child-to-Adult Interactions

Child-to-Adult Interaction Menu Triggers

CATEGORY	INTERACTION	INITIATOR REQUIREMENTS	RECIPIENT REQUIREMENTS
Brag		Daily ≥ 10, Mood ≥ 20	None
Cheer Up		Daily ≥ 5, Mood ≥ 0	Mood ≤ 0
Entertain	Crazy Dance	None	Social ≤ 50
	Handstand	None	Social ≤ 30
	Joke	Mood ≥ 0	None
	Perform Trick	Mood ≥ 10	None
Hug	Nice	Mood ≥ 30, Daily ≥ 30	None
	Friendly	Mood ≥ 35, Daily ≥ 35	None
Insult		Mood ≥ -10, Daily ≥ -5	None
Play	Rock-Paper-Scissors	Mood ≥ 50	None
Talk	Jabber	Daily ≥ 10	None
Tease	Scare	Daily < 10, Mood ≤ -10	None
	Taunt	Daily < 15, Mood ≤ -15	None
Tickle		Mood > 5	None

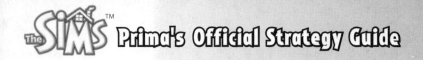

Child-to-Adult Interaction Results

INTERACTION	RESPONSE	DAILY RELATIONSHIP CHANGE	LIFETIME RELATIONSHIP CHANGE	SOCIAL SCORE CHANGE
Brag	Accept	5	0	10
	Reject	-5	-1	0
Be Bragged To	Accept	3	0	5
	Reject	-5	-1	0
Cheer Up	Accept	5	0	7
	Reject	-3	0	0
Be Cheered Up	Accept	10	2	7
	Reject	-10	-2	0
Entertain—Joke	Accept	3	1	9
	Reject	-6	0	0
Be Entertained—Joke	Accept	4	2	10
	Reject	-7	0	0
Entertain—Perform Trick	Accept	3	1	7
	Reject	-5	-1	0
Be Entertained—Perform Trick	Accept	4	2	10
	Reject	-7	-1	0
Entertain—Crazy Dance	Accept	4	2	6
	Reject	-6	-1	0
Be Entertained—Crazy Dance	Accept	3	1	5
	Reject	-5	0	0
Hug—Nice	Accept	4	1	8
	Reject	-5	-1	0
Be Hugged—Nice	Accept	4	1	8
	Reject	-5	-1	0
Hug—Friendly	Accept	5	2	10
	Reject	-10	-3	0
Be Hugged—Friendly	Accept	5	2	10
	Reject	-10	-2	-2
Insult	Accept	-10	-1	5
	Reject	-6	-3	0

Child-to-Adult Interaction Results, continued

INTERACTION	RESPONSE	DAILY RELATIONSHIP CHANGE	LIFETIME RELATIONSHIP CHANGE	SOCIAL SCORE CHANGE
Be Insulted	Accept	-14	-3	-7
	Reject	-12	-5	-10
Play—Rock-Paper-Scissors	Accept	5	1	6
	Reject	-5	-1	-2
Be Played With—Rock-Paper-Scissors	Accept	7	2	6
	Reject	-9	-3	-2
Talk—Jabber	Accept	4	1	5
	Reject	-4	-2	-1
Hear Talk—Jabber	Accept	4	0	5
	Reject	-3	0	0
Tease—Scare	Accept	5	1	10
	Reject	-5	-1	0
Be Teased—Scare	Accept	5	1	8
	Reject	-10	-2	0
Tease—Taunt	Accept	4	0	7
	Reject	-3	0	-3
Be Teased—Taunt	Accept	4	1	7
	Reject	-10	-1	-7
Tickle	Accept	8	1	10
	Reject	-5	-1	0
Be Tickled	Accept	5	1	10
	Reject	-8	-2	0

Child-to-Adult Interaction Success Requirements

CATEGORY	INTERACTION	INITIATOR REQUIREMENTS	RECIPIENT REQUIREMENTS
Brag		Mood ≥ 20, Daily ≥ 10	None
Cheer Up		Mood ≥ 0, Daily ≥ 5	Mood ≤ 0
Entertain	Crazy Dance	None	Social ≤ 0
	Handstand	None	Social ≤ 0
	Joke	Mood ≥ 0	None

Child-to-Adult Interaction Menu Triggers, continued

CATEGORY	INTERACTION	INITIATOR REQUIREMENTS	RECIPIENT REQUIREMENTS
Hug	Nice	Daily $\geq$ 30, Mood > 30	None
	Friendly	Daily $\geq$ 35, Mood > 35	None
Insult		Mood $\leq$ -10	None
		Daily $\leq$ -5	None
Play	Rock-Paper-Scissors	Mood $\geq$ 50	None
Talk	Jabber	Daily $\geq$ 10	None
Tease	Scare	Mood $\leq$ 10	None
		Daily $\leq$ 10	None
	Taunt	Mood $\leq$ 15	None
		Daily $\leq$ 15	None
Tickle		Mood $\geq$ 5	None

Child-to-Child Interactions

Child-to-Child Interaction Success Requirements

CATEGORY	INTERACTION	RECIPIENT REQUIREMENTS
Annoy	Poke	Mood $\geq$ 0, Daily $\geq$ 15
	Push	Mood $\geq$ 0, Daily $\geq$ 10
	Kick Shin	Mood $\geq$ 0, Daily $\geq$ 5
Brag		Daily $\geq$ 20
Cheer Up		Daily $\geq$ 20
Entertain	Joke	Mood $\geq$ 20, Daily > -25
	Perform Trick	Mood $\geq$ 15, Daily $\geq$ -15
Hug	Nice	Mood $\geq$ 20, Daily $\geq$ 10
	Friendly	Mood $\geq$ 20, Daily $\geq$ 10
Insult		Mood > 0, Daily > 20
Play	Rock-Paper-Scissors	Mood $\geq$ 15
	Tag	Mood $\geq$ 15

Child-to-Child Interaction Success Requirements, continued

CATEGORY	INTERACTION	RECIPIENT REQUIREMENTS
Talk	Jabber	Mood ≥ 20, Social ≤ 5
	Whisper	No Data
Tease	Scare	Daily ≥ 30
	Taunt	Daily > 10
		Nice > 3
Tickle		Mood ≥ 25, Daily ≥ 30

Child-to-Child Interaction Results

INTERACTION	RESPONSE	DAILY RELATIONSHIP CHANGE	LIFETIME RELATIONSHIP CHANGE	SOCIAL SCORE CHANGE
Annoy—Push	Accept	-6	-1	6
	Reject	-6	-2	1
Be Annoyed—Push	Accept	-3	-1	6
	Reject	-7	-3	-1
Annoy—Poke	Accept	-4	0	7
	Reject	-4	-1	0
Be Annoyed—Poke	Accept	-2	0	3
	Reject	-5	-1	0
Annoy—Kick Shin	Accept	-8	-2	10
	Reject	-8	-5	2
Be Annoyed—Kick Shin	Accept	-6	-2	9
	Reject	-10	-8	-2
Brag	Accept	5	0	10
	Reject	-5	-1	0
Be Bragged To	Accept	3	0	5
	Reject	-5	-1	0
Cheer Up	Accept	5	0	7
	Reject	-3	0	0
Be Cheered Up	Accept	10	2	7
	Reject	-10	-2	0
Entertain—Joke	Accept	3	1	9
	Reject	-6	0	0

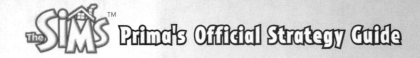

Child-to-Child Interaction Results, continued

INTERACTION	RESPONSE	DAILY RELATIONSHIP CHANGE	LIFETIME RELATIONSHIP CHANGE	SOCIAL SCORE CHANGE
Be Entertained—Joke	Accept	4	2	10
	Reject	-7	0	0
Entertain—Perform Trick	Accept	3	1	7
	Reject	-10	-2	0
Be Entertained—Perform Trick	Accept	4	2	10
	Reject	-7	-1	0
Hug—Nice	Accept	4	1	8
	Reject	-5	-1	0
Be Hugged—Nice	Accept	4	1	8
	Reject	-5	-1	0
Hug—Friendly	Accept	5	2	10
	Reject	-10	-3	0
Be Hugged—Friendly	Accept	5	2	10
	Reject	-10	-2	-2
Insult	Accept	-10	-1	5
	Reject	-6	-3	0
Be Insulted	Accept	-14	-3	-7
	Reject	-12	-5	-10
Play—Rock-Paper-Scissors	Accept	5	1	6
	Reject	-2	-1	0
Be Played With—Rock-Paper-Scissors	Accept	7	2	6
	Reject	-9	-3	-2
Play—Tag	Accept	No Data		
	Reject	No Data		
Be Played With—Tag	Accept	No Data		
	Reject	No Data		
Talk—Jabber	Accept	4	1	5
	Reject	-4	-1	-1
Hear Talk—Jabber	Accept	4	0	5
	Reject	-3	0	0
Tease—Scare	Accept	5	1	10
	Reject	-3	0	0

Child-to-Child Interaction Results, continued

INTERACTION	RESPONSE	DAILY RELATIONSHIP CHANGE	LIFETIME RELATIONSHIP CHANGE	SOCIAL SCORE CHANGE
Be Teased—Scare	Accept	5	1	8
	Reject	-10	1	0
Tease—Taunt	Accept	4	0	7
	Reject	-5	-1	-3
Be Teased—Taunt	Accept	4	1	7
	Reject	-10	2	-7
Tickle	Accept	8	1	10
	Reject	-5	-1	0
Be Tickled	Accept	5	1	10
	Reject	-8	-2	0

Child-to-Child Interaction Menu Triggers

CATEGORY	INTERACTION	INITIATOR REQUIREMENTS	RECIPIENT REQUIREMENTS
Annoy	Poke	Mood ≤ -20	None
	Push	Mood ≤ -10	None
	Kick Shin	Mood ≤ -30	None
Brag		Daily ≥ 10, Mood ≤ 20	None
Cheer Up		Mood ≥ 0	Mood ≤ 0
Entertain	Joke	Mood ≥ 25	None
	Perform Trick	Mood ≥ 25	None
Hug	Nice	Mood ≥ 30, Daily ≥ 30	None
	Friendly	Mood ≥ 35, Daily ≥ 35	None
Insult		Mood ≤ 0	None
		Daily ≤ -10	None
Play	Rock-Paper-Scissors	Mood ≥ 50, Daily ≥ 25	None
	Tag	Mood ≥ 0, Daily ≥ 30	None
Talk	Jabber	Daily ≥ 10	None
	Whisper	Mood ≥ 15, Daily ≥ 15	None
Tease	Scare	Mood ≥ 20	None
		Daily > 0	None
	Taunt	Mood ≤ 15	None
		Daily > 15	None
Tickle		Mood ≥ 5	None

Self Actualization: Interests

Interests are much more robust in *Vacation*, using the same system introduced in *Hot Date*. Interests now have viewable scores, as well as additional topics. The game now includes 15 subjects of interest:

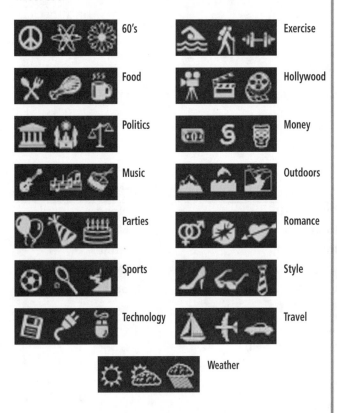

60's	Exercise
Food	Hollywood
Politics	Money
Music	Outdoors
Parties	Romance
Sports	Style
Technology	Travel
Weather	

Each Sim has a set pool of points to divide among all interests. A score of 7 or more in any subject defines high interest, while a score of 3 or less means the Sim is relatively uninterested in that subject. Anything in the remaining range of 4–6 is regarded as moderate interest.

Fig. 10-16. Interests are now plentiful and, better yet, viewable and changeable.

Talk Is Cheap

Instead of generic gab, Sims now talk about their interests. If two conversing Sims share one or more interests at a high level, talking results in maximum gains to their daily relationship score. If the Sims have nothing in common, talking is a waste of time.

> **TIP**
> Use the Ask—About Interests interaction with new acquaintances to figure out what they want to talk about, then change the topic to an interest that your Sim shares.

Use the Talk—Change Subject interaction (available by clicking on your Sim) to steer the conversation toward a common interest or a topic that caters to a particular Sim's interests. This option is only available when your Sim is involved in an ongoing conversation. This interaction is always accepted, so it's a safe play in any situation.

Fig. 10-17. The interest icons displayed above talking Sims represent specific topics of conversation.

CHAPTER 11:
VACATION PLAYGROUNDS

Introduction

Vacation substantially expands the number of objects available in *The Sims*. Newly sorted object lists help you shop with ease for specific types of items. There are more than 140 new objects in the expansion, including some entertaining additions that offer all-new functions and interactions. This chapter introduces you to all of the new objects' features, stats, and functions.

NOTE

All existing player-created objects will be compatible with Vacation, *but any created before the* Hot Date *expansion must be "transmogrified" to work; the object organizer tool allows you to select the catalog information. If you have downloaded objects in your game, you need to get updated copies from* www.thesims.com.

Shop Till You Drop

Each object category now has special sorting options in Buy Mode, making it much easier to browse for a type of object. Instead of digging through all decorations, for example, now you can shop specifically for rugs. This helps you easily compare prices, scores, and design features of similar objects.

Fig. 11-1. Handy new subcategories allow you to sort objects for easy comparison shopping.

You can still shop using the master lists by selecting All at the end of the subcategory listings. However, it's very easy to navigate the subcategory menu, and you'll wonder how you ever did without it after your first shopping trip! It works just like the original menu: click on a subcategory to bring up a sorted list of objects of that type. Use the back arrow to return to the general object categories.

TIP

Hover the mouse over the new subcategory icons to learn what object type they represent. They're very intuitive, so you probably won't need the help after just a few shopping trips.

New Object Types

Vacation gives you much more than just a new set of objects: in this expansion pack, you'll find entirely new types of objects! Midway games, display cases and shelves, rental shacks, and several other new subcategories make your vacations fabulous, adding new touches to your Sims' homes as well. This section looks at each new object type to help you place them with style and use them with success.

Games and Recreation

This object category enjoys some of the greatest expansion in *Vacation*. Your Sims can now play volleyball, take a crack at a snowboarding half pipe, and throw their money into a wide variety of midway games.

Fig. 11-2. Active and playful Sims will love to shred on the new snowboarding half pipe

New Sports

Active Sims will delight in their new choices of sports in *Vacation*. Volleyball, archery, and even snowboarding are a dream come true for your Sims looking to get a little exercise and have fun. Fishing is also available, catering to the more leisure-minded outdoor Sims. The half pipe is available only on Vacation Island, while the archery range and volleyball are available both on the island and downtown.

Three new objects include a special, hidden skill system that determines how well your Sims perform. Archery skill is based on body and logic, while playful Sims excel on the half pipe. These two activities allow your Sim to get better with practice, too. A third object is the Strength O Meter. If the body skill and energy are high, the odds of hitting the slider higher increases, but a tired, weak Sim could hit it higher than a strong, rested Sim.

Arcade Games

You can now build full-fledged arcades, thanks to the addition of the Sim Mars and Seal Team2 upright machines. Both advertise the same high level of fun and are essentially the same, so choose whichever game matches your decor or taste if you're only installing one. For arcade use, mix all three video games in with the pinball machines for a well-equipped fun center, and consider adding some of the midway games described below. You can purchase arcade games for use at home, downtown, or on Vacation Island.

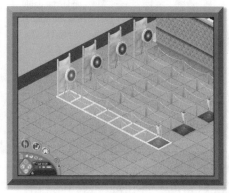

Fig. 11-3. Let your vacationing Sims get a taste of the great outdoors with a little target practice on the archery range.

Volleyball, archery, and fishing are all tied to the rental shack. To give your Sims access to these activities, you need to install two objects. Volleyball requires a volleyball court to host the game and a rental shack to provide the ball (volleyball is also allowed at home). Also, each additional Sim who participates in the game raises the overall level of fun for all Sims playing. Fishing requires a fishing pier from which to cast and the rental shack for gear and tackle. Archers need the archery range and the rental shack for bow and arrow rental. Specific strategies for purchasing and placing these objects are provided in Chapter 12.

CAUTION

There's a one in ten chance each time your Sims play a game that the machine will eat their money. They'll stand at the machine and hit it a few times, to no avail. This experience isn't fun for the Sim, so the best thing to do is feed the machine another Simolean.

TIP

Volleyball is a social game. The more Sims that play in a game, the more fun it is for everyone who participates.

On Vacation Island, you can build forts for play fights using snowballs or water balloons, depending on the climate. These forts are most enjoyed by outgoing Sims. Sims who engage in a snowball fight or water balloon fight gain fun at the expense of comfort and energy. However, these sports don't give body skill.

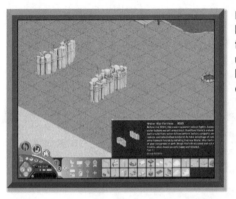

Fig. 11-4. Water balloon fights are fun, but they are understandably hard on your Sims' comfort levels.

Midway Games

The midway games are an entirely new type of object in *The Sims*. These games range from Dart Balloon Toss to the ubiquitous Strength O Meter. These games take Simoleans to play, and Sims are rewarded with tokens depending on their performance. All of the games are fun, with the Chicken Toss and Bust-a-Clown being the most enjoyable. You can place midway games on Vacation Island and downtown, but not at home.

Fig. 11-5. Hurry, hurry, hurry! Step right up and lose your money!

You can redeem the tokens earned in the midway games in a prize booth for special items. you save your tokens for a vacation, any items purchased on Vacation Island with tokens become keepsakes of the trip. These souvenirs have special functionality: they add to the room value at home when placed on display, and they help your Sims remember the vacation. Souvenirs are covered in depth in Chapter 13.

EASTER EGG

There's a special midway game called Whack-a-Will that has an Easter egg, of sorts. The "whackee" is none other than Will Wright, creator of The Sims game. His likeness is on the pop-up targets as well as the bobbing head on a spring at the center of the game table. Also, all of the wacky whacking sound effects are his voice. So whack away if you love *The Sims*.

Fig. 11-6. *The Sims* creator Will Wright makes a special appearance in the Whack-a-Will midway game.

Retail Sales

Sales counters were first introduced in *Hot Date*, and new counters are added in *Vacation*. If you've never played *Hot Date*, you'll experience the new gift system for the first time in *Vacation*. Sims no longer have the Give Gift interaction available by

efault. Instead, they must actually go out and *purchase* a specific gift to have access to the gift-giving interaction. Once purchased, a gift object stays in your Sim's inventory until you choose to give it away.

Fig. 11-7. Now you must *purchase* gifts. Your Sims maintain their own inventories of purchased items to save for that special moment.

To give your Sims access to gifts on vacation, you need a display case and a cash register installed in the same room. Two types of display counters are available in *Vacation*: kitsch and postcards. Kitsch sells what it sounds like: mostly useless junk. These gifts are not souvenirs, but they can be given to other Sims as presents. Postcards are a little more functional. Your Sims can send postcards to their friends and loved ones back home via the mailbox object. These postcards give a small boost to the daily relationship score, which can help your Sims maintain their friendships while they are away on vacation.

Fig. 11-8. Mailing postcards is the only way your vacationing Sims can maintain their friendships with people back home.

To purchase an item, send your Sim over to the display case and select the object you'd like to buy. Find additional information about each object by clicking Browse in the pie menu. Once you've selected an item for purchase, your Sim automatically takes it up to the cash register and pays for it. Once purchased, the item shows up in your Sim's inventory (which you can inspect by clicking on the gift icon in the interface), and then you can give it to another Sim as a relationship-boosting gift.

Souvenir Displays

Souvenir displays are the only new objects specifically designed for use at home. These objects allow your Sims to proudly display the mementos from their vacations. The more souvenirs you have in a display, the more valuable the display is to your room score. Each display holds up to eight souvenirs. When full, a display case acts like an object with a room scorce of eight. Learn more about souvenirs for your home display cases in Chapter 13.

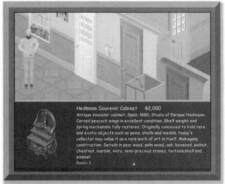

Fig. 11-9. This souvenir display has a special feature: the more souvenirs it displays, the more the peacock's wings spread out!

New Social Objects

Sims have new ways to interact with each other while using objects. Meals have become more interesting, because you can change the topic of conversation at the table to cater to everyone's interests. Vacationing couples and families can build a snowman or a sandcastle together, combining their creativity to make the project more attractive and more fun. Sims can pass the day away lounging on a beach blanket or relaxing in front of a fire on a polar bear rug.

Rental Shack Interactions

The rental shack offers several interactions. Your Sims can rent a picnic basket from the shack and share a nice outdoor meal. If you take the picnic basket to the beach, you'll have the option to rub oil on your date. Your relationship should be fairly good before trying this interaction, and while it does not immediately improve your lifetime relationship, it is a good mood enhancer.

Fig. 11-10. A little tanning oil brings your Sims closer together, while blocking out the sun's harmful rays.

Your Sims can get a wide variety of rental equipment from the rental shack, as described previously in the New Object Types section. Several of the activities associated with these rental objects have unique social interactions available. When a child and adult from the same family are fishing, doing archery, snow sliding, or treasure hunting with each other, the adult may help the child. The chances of these special interactions happening are only about 30–50 percent, but when they happen, they strengthen the relationship. Building a snowman can also result in one of these special situations, in which the adult lifts the child up to place the facial features on the snowman.

Fig. 11-11. Children can share special moments with their parents while they are on vacation.

The snowman and sandcastle sport a new "variable state" system. They can end up in a bad, medium, or good state depending on the creativity of the Sims who build them. While building, the total creativity of everyone who is participating is added, then multiplied by three. So if you were building a snowman with a Sim who had a creativity of 5, his or her total would be 15 because it's counted three times. If a family of four builds a snowman, and everyone has a creativity skill of 2, the overall creativity score would be 24 (2 x 4 x 3). To get the medium state, the overall creativity score must be 24. To get the good state,

the score must be 48. Thus, the more Sims you have working on a snowman or sandcastle, the better it will look.

Keeping the Home Fires Burning

The polar bear rug has some special interactions available for Sims who prefer the cozy indoors. Your Sims can do the same things they can on the picnic blanket, including cuddling and making out. If the rug is in the same room as a lighted fireplace, they can also have a sparkling cider toast, perfect for that romantic getaway moment back at the lodge. The polar bear rug may also be placed at home, allowing your Sims to enjoy the same tender moments in the comfort of their own living room.

Fig. 11-12. There's nothing quite as romantic as a toast in front of the hearth with the Sim of your dreams.

Polar Bear Rug Toast Results

SIM	RESPONSE	DAILY RELATIONSHIP CHANGE	LIFETIME RELATIONSHIP CHANGE	SOCIAL SCORE CHANGE
Initiator	Accept	2	0	5
Initiator	Reject	-3	-1	0
Recipient	Accept	2	0	5
Recipient	Reject	-4	-2	0

New Objects

Dozens of new objects have been added to the game for your decorating and designing pleasure. Chapter 6 already provides you with the definitive buying guide for all of the objects in the game, and you can apply that same information to the new objects listed below. You'll find each object's picture, price, motive values, and distinguishing features in this guide to the new *Vacation* objects.

Seating

Chairs

ReclineTime Pool Chair

§99

Motives: Comfort (2)

NeverFold Camp Chair

§78

Motives: Comfort (2)

Critter Creek Dining Chair

§363

Motives: Comfort (3), Room (1)

Critter Creek Lounger

§611

Motives: Comfort (6), Room (1)

Recliners

Redwood Recliner

§234

Motives: Comfort (3), Energy (1)

ReclineTime Resort Recliner

§109

Motives: Comfort (2), Energy (1)

Eco-Dependency Recliner

§319

Motives: Comfort (3), Energy (1)

Notes: Cuddle interactions are available on this recliner.

Couches

Sew Doe Sofa

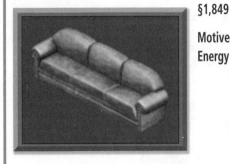

§1,849

Motives: Comfort (9), Energy (5), Room (4)

Beds

The NoTell Motel Bed

§787

Motives: Comfort (8), Energy (8)

Barkworld Sleeper

§2,181

Motives: Comfort (9), Energy (9), Room (1)

Surfaces

Countertops

Sterilife Bathroom Counter

§235

WaveFront Counter

§260

Freedom Counter

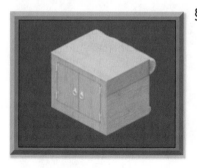

§380

DTS Service Counter

§537

Desks/Tables

ReclineTime Patio Table

§210

Tri-Trunk Coffee Table

§489

Motives: Room (2)

Lawson Bros. "Mountain Table"

§359

Motives: Room (1)

Boomtowne End Table

§142

Chow Sum Phatt Buffet

§254

Motives: Hunger (4)

Decorative

General Decor

Sham-Shag Polar Bear Rug

§9,009

Motives: Room (8)

Notes: Special interactions available if placed in room with fireplace.

Shaker Floor Mirror

§303

Motives: Room (1)

Notes: Allows Sims to build their charisma skill.

Amazin Blazin Jumbo Fireplace

§4,100

Motives: Room (11)

Reflecto Wall Mirror

§329

Notes: Allows Sims to build their charisma skill.

Window Blinds

Revealot Blinds

§75

Obscura Vertical Blinds

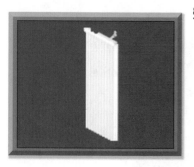

§75

Paintings

"Antique" Sled

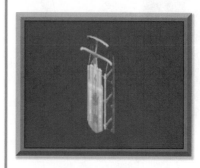

§205

Motives: Room (2)

Vacation Island Inc. Poster

§225

Motives: Room (1)

Souvenir Displays

PhetiShine Curio Cabinet

§896

Motives: Room (2)

ouvenir Wall Cabinet

§234

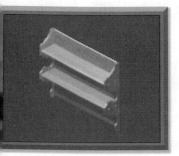

cotillac Wall Cabinet

§487

Motives: Room (2)

dmann Souvenir Cabinet

§2,000

Motives: Room (3)

Mantelpiece Fireplace

§2,525

Motives: Room (8)

Awnings

Sunblind Awning

§173

Fogthwarts Deluxe Awning

§240

Lighting

General Lighting

Octane Drain Camp Lantern

§40

Midnight Bison Table Lamp

§135

Motives: Room (1)

Wall Lights

Conex Wall Sconce

§184

Motives: Room (1)

Skele-Sconce

§225

Motives: Room (1)

Ceiling Lamp

Crumplebottom Chandelier

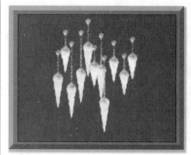

§445

Motives: Room (3)

Plumbing

Redwood Hot Tub

§8,511

Motives: Comfort (5), Hygiene (2), Fun (4)

AquaFluvium Shower-Tub

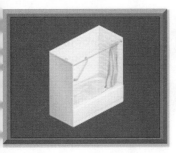

§1,111

Motives: Hygiene (7)

Comfort (3)

Claymore Ceramic Sink

§413

Motives: Hygiene (3)

Miscellaneous

Verm-a-Germ Trash Bin

§39

Paper Recycling Basket

§199

The Wet and Twisted

§419

Jean-ClaucquePost

§1,990

Gluttonator XL BBQ

§299

Motives: Hunger (4)

Arcade Games

Sim Mars

§2,099

Motives: Fun (6)

Notes: Group Activity

ST2 — Barky's Revenge

§2,199

Motives: Fun (6)

Notes: Group Activity

Vacation Island Objects

The following objects are only available for purchase and placement on Vacation Island lots. They won't show up in your neighborhood Buy screens, but some are available in downtown lots if you have *Hot Date*.

Front Desks

Wavefront Hotel Desk

§369

Notes: Spawns clerk.

Lodgepine Lodge Desk

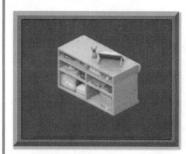

§490

Notes: Spawns clerk.

DTS Hotel Desk System

§570

Notes: Spawns clerk.

Outdoor Accommodations

Intui-Inuit Igloo Site

§579

Motives: Comfort (6), Energy (7)

Sili-Camp Site

§499

Motives: Comfort (6), Energy (7)

Cash Bars

Roxy's Beach Bar

§4,99

Motives: Fun (2)

Notes: Spawns bartender.

Clothing Sales

Surf Tent

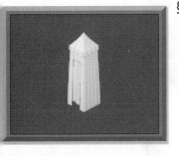

§192

ThermaChange Dressing Booth

§376

Rags-A-Muffin Garmenteria

§3,785

SlopeStyle Skiwear Rack

§5,200

Retail Sales

Snack Stand

§1,984

Motives: Hunger (4)

Tourist Gift Center

§3,000

Postcard Center

§794

Bayes "InvenStory" Register

§229

Notes: Spawns clerk.

Sports and Recreation

Archery Range

§779

Motives: Fun (5)

Notes: To use the archery range there must be a rental shack.

Fishing Pier

§888

Motives: Fun (5)

Notes: To use the fishing pier there must be a rental shack.

Frost Fortress

§515

Motives: Fun (4)

Notes: Group Activity

Blaäanko Super Pipe

§8,439

Motives: Fun (9)

Rental Shed "Au Naturel"

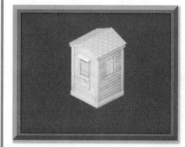

§2,012

Notes: Spawns clerk.

Volleyball Court

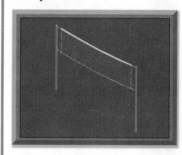

§120

Motives: Fun (6)

Notes: To use the volleyball court there must be a rental shack. Can also be purchased/used at home.

Water War Fortress

§565

Motives: Fun (4)

Notes: Group Activity

Ice Ape Snow Slide

§7,439

Motives: Fun (8)

Midway Games

Chicken Toss

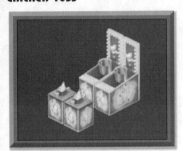

§2,483

Motives: Fun (6)

Captain Popper's Dart Game

§1,599

Motives: Fun (4)

Prize Booth

§4,766

Bust-A-Clown Game

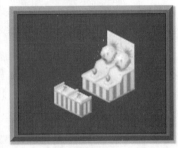

§3,110

Motives: Fun (5)

Strength O Meter

§1,950

Motives: Fun (3)

Whack-a-Will

§3,999

Motives: Fun (7)

CHAPTER 12:
PAVING OVER PARADISE

Introduction

In *Vacation*, you build on the all-new Vacation Island, which is completely different from the usual neighborhood lots. Your vacation getaways can include resort hotels, outdoor games and leisure activities, shops, restaurants, and other retreats. This chapter teaches you how to create a vacation lot that rewards your Sims with the best time they've had since you built their house!

Fig. 12-1. The plane! The plane! My dear guests, *welcome* to Vacation Island.

Setting the Scene

Vacation Island lots use the same Build and Buy Mode tools that you're familiar with from building your Sims' houses. However, there are a few differences in both form and function in the menus and objects, and vacation lots require a different planning strategy than homes. This section examines how to create your vacation paradise.

Planning for Paradise

Your Sims behave differently while on vacation, and the satisfaction availability for the motives changes. Approach building a vacation lot with different strategies than you use on your Sims' home lots. At home, your Sims spend a great deal of time at work or school, which takes them out of action for several hours a day. On vacation, they engage in various activities all day. Find new ways of satisfying their basic needs; the bathrooms are public (except "room" bathrooms), the fridge is nowhere to be seen, and there are better things to do than watch TV on vacation!

The first thing to remember is money. Almost everything the Sims do costs money, yet they don't have to purchase the items they use. New types of objects that are only available on vacation lots further separate your island lots from your familiar neighborhoods. This section helps you make the transition from residential building to resort planning.

Fig. 12-2. The concept of an all-inclusive resort changes your basic building strategy.

Feeling Groovy

While your Sims are on vacation, they benefit from reduced rates of decay in some motives, allowing them to enjoy themselves for longer periods without having to attend to personal upkeep. Comfort and energy loss are slowed, and if your Sims are in a good mood, they experience a lower rate of fun decay. Your Sims are relieved of all concerns for maintenance, cleanup, and other household chores, allowing you to concentrate on showing them a good time.

The motive bonuses mean you should change the balance of your object selections on a vacation lot. Bladder, hunger, hygiene, and room are your target motives. Social needs are important, but your Sims have ample opportunity to hobnob with other Sims on vacation. The special *Vacation* objects are mainly social activities, and you'll meet random non-player character (NPC) tourists on the island.

Fig. 12-3. It's paradise: new Sims to befriend on the island, and no chance of getting voted off!

Build a dining room for your resort guests, centered around one or more buffet tables. The resort staff keeps the buffet stocked with food for free, allowing your Sims to freely graze Use the most comfortable chairs in the dining area; this maximizes your Sims' eating time with a solid boost to their comfort motives.

Fig. 12-4. Free meals around the clock are a dream come true for some Sims.

Place bathrooms near your dining room for handiness after a meal, and they should provide ample access. You'll want more than one bathroom on a vacation lot, because it accommodates NPC Sims as well as your vacation party. If the bathrooms get too congested, accidents can happen, ruining the mood of even the best vacation day. Make your bathrooms accessible to several Sims at once; they should be large enough inside for Sims to get around each other.

Resort Investment

When building your world-class resort, you have unlimited spending power. Items that are far out of your family's reach in their homes can be purchased without a second thought on your vacation lots. At home, you consider the cost of each item you place, as the money comes directly from your Sims' limited savings pool. Conversely, make style, size, and motive value your primary considerations when buying for resorts, since money is no object.

Fig. 12-5. Splurge on big-ticket items in your resorts, allowing your Sims to enjoy some of life's finer pleasures while on vacation.

Use your financial freedom to max out your room scores. Spend thousands on the decorative objects you can't afford at home; their strategic placement adds greatly to your Sims'

room scores. Higher room scores improve your Sims' overall mood scores, which are the basic measure of how successful your vacations are. If your Sims are in consistently good moods, you can take home one of the super souvenirs described in Chapter 13.

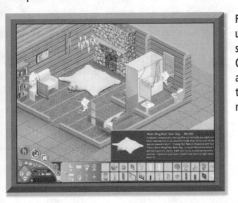

Fig. 12-6. With an unlimited budget, splurge on decor. Create pleasant areas in your resort to maximize your mood scores.

New Building Elements

The *Vacation* expansion includes dozens of additional building elements, such as new floors, tiles, and walls specifically themed for woodland lodges and beachside resorts. You'll also find all-new types of building elements—additional ways to shape your Sims' world.

New Fencing

Several new dividers and fences are in your building tools. Some new fence elements form archways between two columns set in a straight line, two squares apart. You can create three- and four-way junctions, allowing you to design beautiful outdoor structures, patios, and breezeways, or add an elegant touch to indoor galleries.

Fig. 12-7. Balloons tied into archways add a special festive feeling at home or on vacation.

The modern fence has a special feature. When several are laid together, they form end caps and intermediate posts, creating an attractive finished look. These fences help define outdoor spaces, dividing your lots into sections. Plan for periodic breaks in walls so that your Sims don't have to walk around a continuous wall just to get a few squares away.

> ### VACATION-ONLY OBJECTS
>
> Several of the new items included in *Vacation* can only be placed on vacation lots; you won't see them on your household Build menus. These objects are listed in Chapter 11's object lists, so refer to that chapter if you can't find one of the new objects in your home Build menu.

Resort Planning

Your Sims are going on vacation to spend several days in the same place, sharing it with dozens of other Sims. These factors make your resort layout even more important than your home layout, as your traffic areas have to accommodate more Sims, and your overall lot has to cater to all of your Sims' needs. This section outlines some of the specific considerations for constructing an enjoyable, efficient resort.

Traffic Flow

Like *Hot Date*'s downtown area, vacation lots must accommodate large groups of Sims competing for the same space. Huge crowds share the same dining tables, restrooms, recreational facilities, and ground space with your Sims. Make sure everyone can get where they want to go without having to take the long way around. Pay attention to traffic flow.

Fig. 12-8. Narrow hallways are disastrous on a vacation lot.

A good traffic corridor is at least three squares wide on a public lot. That's 50 percent bigger than the proper corridor width at home. You'll frequently encounter more than two Sims passing through the same point in a hall or tight area, but you will seldom see more than four competing for the same space at the same time.

Inspect your lot for hot spots. These locations offer unique or important services to all Sims on the lot. Bathrooms, buffet tables, bars, and the only ladder out of a pool are places where Sims bunch up. Relieve these hot spots by building additional facilities. Two separate bathrooms on different ends of the lot, two buffet tables on opposite sides of the dining hall, and multiple entrances and exits from all heavy-use areas will help relieve hot spots. In cases where duplicate facilities are undesirable, keep a four-square radius around the interaction location clear. This allows

Sims waiting in line to stack up and still lets other Sims pass through the area. This sacrifices space efficiency, but serves your lots well in actual play.

> **TIP**
> *Test your vacation lots with practice runs. Take one of your Sims on a vacation to see how well your areas work. When you finish, quit the game without saving so that you don't affect your guinea Sim.*

All-in-One Destinations

Every vacation lot is like a single home lot in the neighborhood. Each of your resort lots are all-in-one vacation destinations, with the ability to serve every Sim's motive need. Don't wait until your family is on vacation to discover that your ocean paradise doesn't have a bathroom! Focus on making one lot perfect before spreading your creativity across the entire island. This saves your Sims time, energy, and money when they arrive, relieving them of the need to hop a shuttle to other parts of the island every day.

Fig. 12-9. Don't drink the water—in fact, try not to drink anything, since there are no bathrooms!

Your vacation lots should fit together as a complementary whole. Sims have varying reactions to objects and interactions based on their personalities. Your active Sims might be eager to find a

resort with volleyball, a pool slide, and a water balloon fight, but the same resort might be a nightmare for your lazy Sims! Balance all lots within themselves; you can tailor each lot to a specific personality type.

> ## TIP
> *Your vacation lots benefit from the inclusion of some* Hot Date *objects, as well as others from previous expansion packs. Install the other Sims expansions to increase your building options.*

You can build vacation destinations that serve the varying needs of each Sim in your neighborhood. Go heavy on fishing, lounging, and treasure hunting on one lot, making it the best choice for lazy Sims. Center another lot around snowboarding, midway games, an arcade, and other attractions that appeal to playful Sims. Each lot should still serve all interests, but develop each with a particular set of interests or personalities in mind. This way you avoid creating generic, cover-all lots, and you provide real and meaningful choices for your Sims.

Fig. 12-10. Structure resorts that specialize in attracting particular types of Sims.

Frame Rates

Consider video display frame rates when building vacation lots. At home, your computer tracks the animations, moods, and autonomous decisions for your family members. On vacation lots, your computer does the same thing for all of the NPC Sims on vacation as well. Each animated object you place downtown affects your computer's video processing power. The more animation you have on the screen at the same time, the slower the game moves. Unless your computer has a lot of horsepower (or if you intend to post your downtown lots on the Sims Exchange), keep down the number of animated objects.

Building for Success

Vacation includes special new types of buildings that have specific requirements. In addition to having specific objects to complete a fully operational attraction, you must carefully plan your rooms, spaces, and passages to allow for maximum functionality. This section helps you create all of the new attractions and building types.

Fig. 12-13. Imagine our Sims' discouragement when they discover that the hotel has no vacancy because there are no beds!

When you're building your Sim's home, you can sacrifice function for form. You control everyone in the house (other than the occasional guest) at home, so you can solve traffic jams with a few simple "Go here" clicks. On vacation, however, you only have control over a few of the Sims. If a traffic jam develops (or someone is hogging the only space at the bar, for example), you're out of luck. Therefore, function is the most important factor when building downtown.

Dining Halls

Your Sims eat for free on vacation, thanks to the 24-hour, all-you-can-eat buffet. Unfortunately, other Sims compete with yours for dining real estate, and some are bold enough to cut in line at the buffet! Install adequate dining space and allow plenty of passing room in the dining area. Install at least 12 easily accessed dining table seats on any one lot—more if you plan to take more than one Sim on vacation. Dining halls have only three requirements for successful construction:

- **Buffet table**
- **Dining table**
- **Dining chairs**

Traffic flow near your buffet table is very important, because eating is one of downtown Sims' favorite activities. Leave three to five squares of open space around your buffet tables to allow for maximum flow to and from the food. Place two buffet tables in a room, either in a long row down the center of the room or side by side, separated by about three squares. Do not place them adjacent to each other, because this causes traffic congestion.

Fig. 12-14. A pair of buffet tables helps expedite the dining experience for your Sims.

Seating is another important concern in dining halls. Provide your Sims with comfortable seating while dining to serve their comfort motives. Meals can go on for several hours of Sim time, so make the most of the experience. Max out your room score around the tables with ample decorations, and include good lighting coverage. With hunger, comfort, room, and social guaranteed to be at high scores during dinner, your Sims have the best chance to maintain a good mood. As a result, they have more successful mood-dependent interactions during and after their meals.

Fig. 12-15. Set up your Sims for success at meal time with objects that serve all of their motives.

When you're decorating your dining area, pay attention to the seating arrangements during meals. Don't place objects where they obstruct your Sims' faces or the thought bubbles above their seats. These objects prevent you from

viewing your Sims when they are eating, which can be frustrating. Hanging plants and ceiling lights are the most common obstructions, but wall objects such as paintings, sconces, and tapestries can also obstruct your view.

Shops

You can set up tourist traps—er, retail shops—to sell trinkets. After purchase, your Sims can give these trinkets as gifts. *Vacation* uses the new gift system introduced in *Hot Date*. Now, you've got to go out and buy those treasures to give to your Sim sweetheart! Shops require only two elements to work properly:

- **Cash register**
- **Sales rack or display**

Of course, it's nice to have more than one sales rack. Several varieties of each kind of retail display are available, although some sell the same type of items. Mix and match your retail displays for the best visual appearance, but, as with a dining hall, it's important to keep your shop's hot spots in mind. The cash register and the entrances and exits to your shop are focal points. Standing displays can be roadblocks, so either place them against walls or allow for ample aisle space between them.

Fig. 12-16. Leave plenty of space between your retail displays for browsing tourists.

> **TIP**
> One register can cover several stores, so long as they are in the same continuous room. However, you shouldn't skimp on registers, or your Sims will have to walk too far to complete their purchases.

Bars

The cabana bar is a fun new object that builds on the bars introduced in *Hot Date*. The fizzy bubbles in the bar drinks tickle Sim noses, putting them in a better mood and making them more likely to accept various relationship-dependent interactions! The cabana bar is one of the easiest facilities to build. However, it is one of the hardest facilities to build *right*, as the special traffic demands and its popularity with the Sims make the bar a very crowded hot spot. All you need to build a bar is the bar object itself and an associated counter:

- **Bar**
- **Counter**

The hard part comes in planning for the traffic your bar generates. You can easily find a dozen Sims ponied up to the bar at once, making ordering a nightmare. Build long bars—at least six countertops laid in a line. Box in your bartenders with a side counter so that patrons can't get behind the bar and block their access to the cash register (don't worry, they'll hop over the counter after last call).

Fig. 12-17. Make sure the bartender has unfettered access to the all-important cash register by closing off access behind the bar.

- Rental shack
- Fishing pier
- Basketball hoop
- Volleyball court
- Swimming pool
- Park bench, garden swing
- Barbecue and picnic table
- Archery range
- Bathroom facilities

You can also create tables in your bar, which spawn a barmaid for table service. Use any mix of dining tables and chairs to suit your preferences and decor. Create a completely open space between the seating area and the bar, where the barmaid will return for the drinks ordered by seated Sims. The traffic corridor should be almost as wide as the bar itself and should provide direct access to all of the tables.

Don't forget to attend to your park's room score. Ample landscaping can create an idyllic outdoor location for your Sims. Trees are a necessity, of course. Fountains and statues add to the visual appeal as well, although these should be used in moderation to avoid a cluttered look. Remember to install lighting if you want your Sims to enjoy the park after dark.

CAUTION

If the route from the bar seating to the service bar is too cluttered, the barmaid gets slowed down by counter patrons, reducing her service time to a crawl. Keep that path clear to keep the drinks coming!

Other Diversions

The midway is one of the most entertaining new additions. Your Sims accumulate prize tokens from the midway games, which you can turn in for prizes at the prize booth. These prizes actually count as souvenirs, and as such they contribute to your overall vacation score. Vacation score is covered fully in Chapter 13—if you get it high enough, your Sims take home an extra-special souvenir to remember their vacation. To build a midway, you need the following objects:

- **One or more midway games**
- **Prize booth**

Parks

Parks and recreational areas are a great way for your Sims to spend some quality time together. Active Sims enjoy attractions like volleyball and basketball courts, swimming pools, and archery, while lazy Sims can spend a quiet afternoon on a picnic blanket or fishing. There are no specific requirements for building a park, but the following items provide your Sims with something to do besides watching grass grow.

Create a child's paradise by mixing in video games with your midway attractions, creating the ultimate arcade.

Fig. 12-18. A dance hall nightclub is a great addition to any resort that hosts exuberant young Sims on vacation.

Don't forget the nightlife! Try building a dance club for your hip and fly Sims to party late into the night. If you have the *House Party* expansion, you can make excellent use of many of the party objects included therein. Many of the *House Party* objects offer group activities that allow your Sims to improve their relationships while catering to one or more motives.

CHAPTER 13:
GETTING AWAY FROM IT ALL

Introduction

All of the elements of the *Vacation* expansion come together when you take your Sims on a getaway to Vacation Island. This chapter helps you plan and execute the perfect holiday for your Sims, whether you're packing for an overnighter or an extended stay in an exotic locale. You'll learn how to keep your Sims entertained on vacation, manage their finances, and look after their every need. This chapter also tells you what to expect on vacation and how to excel at the special vacation challenges and hidden opportunities.

Booking a Vacation

All Sim vacations begin with a phone call. As long as your Sims have 500 Simoleans in the bank, the Call Cab—Go on Vacation option shows up in the telephone pie menu. Note that only adults can make vacation reservations, so little Tommy can't make the call. Once the call is made, you have about 15 minutes of Sim time to finish anything that's happening in the house before the vacation shuttle arrives. Then, the family piles into the truck and heads off.

Fig. 13-1. A new option in the phone pie menu allows adults to book a vacation for the whole family.

You can also go on vacation with a Sim who doesn't live on your home lot. Have your Sim call the friend, then choose Invite on Vacation from the phone call pie menu. If the friend accepts, the vacation shuttle shows up just for the Sim who issued the invitation, and the two Sims arrive on Vacation Island together. These getaways have some special features associated with them, and they are covered in the "Vacations for Two" sidebar.

NOTE

You cannot limit your vacation party to specific Sims in one household. When you book a vacation, all Sims on the lot automatically go with you. If one or more of your Sims are away at work or school when you call, the travel agent advises you to call back when the whole family is home.

VACATIONS FOR TWO

You can take one of your Sims on vacation using the Invite on Vacation phone call. This essentially sets up a vacation "date," very similar to the dates in the *Hot Date* expansion. While your duo is vacationing, a purple plumb appears over your partner's head at all times, identifying your holiday buddy. You won't have direct control, but your partner will follow your Sim's lead and engage in the same activities whenever possible.

All fees incurred on vacation are charged to the Sim who initiated the vacation, so be ready to shoulder the expenses. Keep tabs on the needs of your vacation partner by choosing Ask—About Needs. This tells you what your partner needs most at the moment, allowing you to choose an activity that caters to the lowest motive score. The main difference between a downtown date and a Vacation Island date is that you can't Say Good-bye to a vacation partner. You're stuck together until you end the vacation by calling for the shuttle to take you and your guest home. Note that your date must be in a "love" relationship to sleep in the same igloo as you, otherwise, neither person will rest and you'll need to take them to a hotel.

Packing and Planning

When you leave the house, everything is saved exactly as it is. Your Sims will return at the same Sim time that they left, and they'll still have their jobs, school, and home upkeep to contend with when they get back. To avoid jet lag, try sending your family on vacation in the middle of the day, after skipping work and school. Simply cancel their actions when the bus or carpool arrives, and they'll stay home for the day. Any Sim can take one day off of work or school without getting in trouble—just don't do it two days in a row, or your Sim will be out of a job.

Your Sims arrive on Vacation Island bright and early in the morning, so they have a whole day in front of them. Therefore, nurse their energy levels by taking a midmorning nap on a couch, or at least by avoiding any energy-sapping activities like playing, working out, or excessive walking. They'll then have enough energy to get through their first day on vacation. When they return from vacation, take the second half of the day to recover their motive scores before sending them off to work and school the following morning.

Fig. 13-2. Have your Sims relax on the morning of their vacation, so they'll have enough energy for the upcoming fun.

Arriving on the Island

After your family has boarded the cruise ship, decide what vacation lot to visit. Base your decision on the personalities of your vacationing Sims and the lots that you've built. If you're using the default vacation lots, send playful people to the beach, active people to the mountains, and lazy people to the woods. Really, any of the default lots work fine for any Sim, so if you have a preference, go for it. Also, your Sims are free to change lots while they're on vacation, so the decision isn't a binding one.

Fig. 13-3. You can choose any lot that suits your fancy, although some lots excel at serving the needs and interests of specific personality types.

Once you've selected a vacation lot, the shuttle drops off your family at the chosen resort. Send an adult Sim to the front desk to reserve a room, allowing all of your Sims access to any of the bedrooms on the lot. Once you've checked in, the NPCs stay out of these bedrooms, giving you uncontested access to the bathrooms, beds, and other amenities. You don't have to choose just one bedroom after checking in; essentially, you get the entire resort to yourself for one bargain price.

Fig. 13-4. Checking into a room at the front desk gives your Sims exclusive access to all of the bedrooms on the lot.

If your Sims are adventurous, rent a tent instead of a room. Roughing it in the great outdoors can be fun, and your Sims can all help pitch the tent. The more Sims who contribute to setting up the tent, the better it will be. As with the snowman and sandcastle activities described in

Chapter 11, all Sims involved in the building contribute three times their creativity. If the total creativity is 24 or more, you'll get a mediocre tent. To reach the good state, the score must be 48. Below 24, your living quarters are going to be pretty dilapidated.

Making New Friends

Once you're checked into the resort, you're ready to begin your vacation in earnest. You'll notice other Sims sharing the resort with you. These are a mix of randomly generated characters and special NPC employees of the resort. This section describes both types.

New Faces

A diverse cast of randomly generated characters will show up on the island. These NPCs are generated by mixing and matching the bodies and outfits in the skins folder. Their personalities, interests, and even moods are also random, so you'll probably find an NPC who's perfectly matched for a friendship (or romance) with any one of the Sims in your neighborhood. These random Sims go about their own vacations just like your Sims.

Fig. 13-5. Establishing a relationship with one of the NPCs adds him or her to your Sim's relationship bar.

If you don't interact with random Sims, they simply disappear. On the other hand, if you establish any kind of relationship with a random Sim, that NPC (whose face is added to your relationships bar) is "locked" and saved. Once this happens, that NPC becomes a permanent Sim in your game, allowing an ongoing relationship. These NPCs won't show up in any of your neighborhood lots on their own, but you can call them and invite them over. If you actually get to the point where you Propose or ask the Sim to Move In, your family gains a new member, who behaves like an original member of your Sim neighborhood.

Meet the Help

You meet several new types of NPC staff on the island, ranging from the highly interactive vacation director to the shy housekeeping maid. Each NPC has a specific task, and understanding their functions and motives will help your Sims enjoy themselves while on vacation.

Vacation Director Kana

Kana introduces herself almost as soon as you arrive on the island. She's a font of vacation knowledge, and you can ask her questions about anything relating to your vacation activities. Kana is also in charge of making sure everyone at her resort is guaranteed a good time. This means she'll be keeping an eye on your Sim children, and if they get out of line you'll be

hearing from her! Child discipline is covered thoroughly in the section "Keep Those Kids in Line."

> # NOTE
>
> *The vacation director is modeled after a certain real-life producer at Maxis, the company that created* The Sims.

The Maid

The maid is on duty around the clock, cleaning messes, busing dishes, and keeping on top of the resort's general upkeep. She's usually very busy just busing tables, although she also tidies the bedrooms from time to time. Your Sims can't interact with her, so don't bother trying to ask for more towels or combination shampoo-conditioner.

Fig. 13-6. The maid is usually busy busing tables at the buffet.

You can help the maid when you are building lots by installing a dishwasher very close to the eating areas. This gives her somewhere to drop off dirty dishes produced by the resort guests without sending her all the way to a bathroom sink. If a dishwasher is out of place in your resort, a simple sink placed nearby can serve the same function.

The Janitor

Janitors are a staple of any resort, and they appear automatically. They don't provide you with any direct interaction, but they can often be anything from an amusement to a nuisance as they go from room to room cleaning, oblivious to the activities of the Sims around them. Avoid trapping a janitor in a hallway or room you want to use, or your vacation shenanigans could stall as your Sim tries to get around the sanitation engineer.

Retail Clerks

When you've selected something for purchase from a retail rack, your Sim will take the item to the register and pay the cashier. Other than that, clerks are generally uninterested in helping you shop.

Front Desk Clerks

Front desk clerks stand behind the hotel desk, eager to book your Sims into a room for the night. Click on the desk rather than the clerk in order to check in.

> **NOTE**
>
> Smart criminals don't mix business with pleasure, so don't expect your professional criminal to pull off shoplifting. Criminal masterminds have to pay for their selections in the stores while on vacation just like other Sims, saving the larceny for when they're on the job. So relax, have fun, and spend a few of those hard-stolen Simoleans on your vacation.

Rental Shack Attendant

The rental shack attendant intermittently mans the equipment-rental facilities at the resorts. He's a voyeur, slow on the uptake and quick to take a break. Click on the shack to rent equipment, and he'll help you when he feels like it.

> **TIP**
>
> If you're on vacation with a frisky sweetheart, watch for the attendant to leave the shack for a break. While he's gone, sneak into the shack for a little romp in public! This hidden maneuver can turn your vacation into a very steamy holiday.

The Bartender

Placing a bar on your lot automatically creates a bartender, who serves up the drinks. Wait in line when the bar is crowded, and you'll be served in turn. You can't interact with the bartenders. Drinking at the bar improves the success rate of some interactions.

The Barmaid

When a room contains a bar and one or more tables with chairs, a barmaid is spawned. You may click on the barmaid and order a drink. Your Sim stays seated, and the barmaid comes over, gets your drink order, retrieves it from the bar, and then delivers it to your table. This is an excellent way to patronize a bar, as your Sims benefit from the comfort of sitting while they wait for and enjoy their drinks.

Fig. 13-7. The barmaid comes to your Sim's table to take a beverage order.

Resort Theme Characters

Each resort employs a special theme character to delight the kiddies and create those magical scrapbook photo opportunities. Each resort's theme character is in keeping with the physical setting. Beach resorts employ the entertaining Marky Shark.

Marky Shark

Archie Archer

Betty Yeti

You'll find Archie Archer at the forest resorts, eager to put you in the mood for a little target practice on the archery range.

The snowy climes of the mountain resorts are plied by the infamous Betty Yeti, so keep your cameras ready!

You can't initiate interactions with the theme characters, but they'll drop by and give your Sims a wave—or a scare!

Power Vacationing

The focus of your vacations can be anything you want it to be: seeing new places, getting out of the house, building relationships, or any other goal you have in mind. However, Sims who take their vacations seriously can be eligible for some very hefty rewards. Give your Sims the best vacation ever by achieving some of the game's concrete goals.

Fig. 13-9. Keep your Sims' moods up to earn vacation score points four times a day.

Fig. 13-8. Tender moments like building a snowman together can help your family earn a super souvenir.

Vacation Score

Your Sims accrue a hidden number called a vacation score, which tracks all of their activities, fun, successes, and failures. If your Sims get a high enough score by the time they return home, they receive a special reward called a super souvenir.

Setting the Mood for Success

The vacation score is based on your Sims' average mood each day and their specific activities on vacation. Four times a day, your Sims' moods are averaged and recorded. This happens at 6 a.m., noon, 6 p.m., and midnight. If the average mood of your adult Sims is greater than about two green bars, your vacation score goes up 6 points. You get another 3 points if your child Sims are also averaging a mood of 40 or better at these times. Thus, two adults and one child all above mood 40 add 9 points to your vacation score each time they are checked. Bad moods have the opposite effect: adults at 0 or less drop the vacation score by 2, and children do the same.

Fun and Finds

Special finds also add to your vacation score. If your Sims find a relic souvenir while fishing or treasure hunting with the metal detector, 10 points are added to your score. Winning tokens on the midway games results in a 25 percent chance of earning 1 point. Catching a fish can help, with 2 points awarded for landing one on the pier. Just having fun helps your vacation score as well. Your Sims earn 2 points each time they build a snowman or sandcastle.

Keep Those Kids in Line

Kids double your chances of earning mood-based vacation points, but they're also a liability. If you allow their moods to slip too low, they start to exhibit deviant behavior. This starts with harmless idling like chain burps and moronic wailing, but soon they engage in property destruction and aggressive outbursts.

> **TIP** Have one of your adult Sims scold a child who misbehaves. If successful, it strengthens their relationship and helps deter future acts by raising the child's mood.

Vacation director Kana will advise you that your children must behave according to the resort standards. Your Sims are fined for the misbehavior, in compensation for damages done. These incidents hurt your vacation score to the tune of −10 points. Worse yet, if your Sims get three warnings, they'll be tossed off the island and sent back home without a refund! Pay special attention to children who are acting up, and fulfill their motive needs to improve their moods immediately.

Fig. 13-10. Deviant behavior from the children can sabotage a vacation.

The Final Tally

At the end of your vacation, your vacation score is tallied. If you earned more than 150 points, Kana informs you that you've had such a memorable visit that you've earned a special super souvenir. The type depends on the kind of vacation lot you're leaving. You earn a golden pine cone in the woods, a golden sun on the beach, or a snow globe in the snowy mountains. Note that it doesn't matter where you spent the majority of your vacation time; your super souvenir matches the lot from which you place the call to go home.

Souvenirs

Your Sims can purchase and find special mementos called souvenirs. These treasured items can only be acquired on the island, and they are very valuable to a Sim household. Souvenirs in the home add to the room score of the room, and they have some special interactions available.

There are three basic kinds of souvenirs: those purchased in the prize booth, those found while treasure hunting or fishing, and super souvenirs awarded for high vacation scores.

Souvenirs

SOUVENIR	RESALE VALUE	SOURCE
Arrowhead	§464	Treasure Hunt
Baby Doll	§13	Prize Booth
Black Lava Idol	§173	Treasure Hunt
Ceramic Chicken Cookie Jar	§92	Prize Booth
Coconut Monkey	§25	Prize Booth
Fertility God	§243	Treasure Hunt, Fishing
Golden Llama	§288	Prize Booth
Golden Pine Cone	§502	Super Souvenir
Golden Sun	§633	Super Souvenir
Guinea Pig	§111	Prize Booth
Old Boot	§3	Treasure Hunt, Fishing
Penguin	§101	Prize Booth
Pirate Chest	§99	Treasure Hunt, Fishing
Quartz Skull	§188	Treasure Hunt, Fishing
Snow Globe	§551	Super Souvenir
Wood Squirrel	§65	Prize Booth

Souvenirs that you can buy are available in the prize booth. To purchase them, your Sims must earn game tokens from the midway games. Save your tokens from one vacation to another, or even earn tokens downtown and redeem them for souvenirs. While this won't help your vacation score, you can amass many souvenirs for display at home.

Found souvenirs can only be acquired by using a metal detector (available at the rental shack) or while fishing. You can find all of the souvenirs using the metal detector, but you can only find some of the treasures while fishing.

Fig. 13-11. Find souvenirs while searching with a metal detector or fishing off the pier.

The super souvenirs are awarded by Kana for outstanding vacation scores, and they are the most valuable. Achieve a vacation score of more than 150 by the time you leave, and your Sims are awarded a super souvenir as described previously in the "Vacation Score" section.

Souvenirs at Home

Your Sims automatically place any souvenirs they bring home in a souvenir display case, if you have one. Otherwise, they are placed on any available surface. Each souvenir has a memory associated with it, which your Sims can recall whenever they handle the item. The Sim's mood is recorded at the moment the item is acquired. Once home, any Sim can use the object to remember the moment it was acquired for a boost in fun. If the Sim was in a good mood when the object was gained, the Sim doing the remembering gestures pleasantly. If the object was acquired while the recipient was in a bad mood, the Sim's reaction is unpleasant. Even bad memories, however, are enjoyable to remember (just think of all the times you've traded stories with your friends about "the worst time you ever had").

Sims can make remembering a social event, as well. If there are other Sims in the room when a Sim reminisces with a souvenir, the Sim tells them the story associated with the item. This interaction adds to everyone's social motive, and it is fun for everyone listening as well. Remembering or listening adds 10 fun points, plus 35 social points if it is done with an audience. You can watch your Sim use animated gestures and articulation to describe the events surrounding the souvenir's acquisition for a few minutes of Sim-time.

Souvenirs are valuable just sitting in a room, as well. Prize booth souvenirs add 1 point to the room score, found souvenirs add 2 points, and super souvenirs add 3 full points to the room score of the room in which you display them. If you display them in a dedicated souvenir display case that contains the maximum eight souvenirs, that case acts like an object with a room score of eight.

Rest and Relaxation

With the vacation score and souvenirs in mind, it's time to let your Sims loose to enjoy themselves in the luxury and tamed splendor of Vacation Island. This section looks at some of the more enticing activities for vacationers. Your overall objective is to maintain high mood scores for all of your Sims by serving all of their motive needs equally and fully. We examine the various motives you'll be satisfying in the following sections.

Energy and Comfort

These two motives are perhaps the hardest to keep up while on vacation. Many of the activities on Vacation Island incorporate heavy exertion or long periods of time spent standing up, both of which can take a toll on comfort and energy levels.

Fig. 13-12. It can be hard to maintain a high energy level when your Sims engage in athletic activities.

Appropriate attire is critical to your Sims' comfort levels while they are on vacation. Heavy parkas on the beach certainly won't make anyone happy, while bathing suits at the ski resort make for a very disgruntled Sim-cicle. Use dressing booths to change your Sims into outfits that suit the climate at the part of the island you're visiting.

Tent sleeping is cheap, and the novelty of watching your Sims roughing it is undeniably fun. Unfortunately, sleeping on the cold, hard ground isn't nearly as restful as curling up in a warm room on a pillow-top bed, and your Sims will suffer for it the following day. If you can afford it and it suits your vacation plans, consider renting a room in the lodge instead of pitching a tent. This helps your Sims maximize their comfort and energy levels before facing another wild day of vacationing.

Fig. 13-13. Sleeping under the stars sounds fun, but your Sims will be a little worse for wear in the morning.

Help your Sims conserve energy throughout the day by pacing their activities. Don't send them on a wild series of sports activities without a nice break in between. Give them a chance to sit and rest in between snowboarding runs, or even allow them to take a nap in the middle of the day. Don't let them stand around idly for any unnecessary length of time, as this doesn't help any of their motives and takes away from their comfort and energy. Have your Sims sit if they must pass some time before their next activity.

Give your Sims good seating at mealtime, so that they can recharge their comfort scores while they gobble down all that buffet food. Since you aren't paying for your furnishings at the resorts, splurge when you're building your dining areas and install the most comfortable chairs you can. If there isn't room at any of the choice tables when

ou are thinking about sending your Sims through
he buffet line, wait until the dining hall clears out
 little. The worst thing to do at mealtime is to
end your Sims to eat when there isn't any seating
vailable. They'll eat standing up, wasting their
nergy and becoming decidedly uncomfortable in
he process.

Fig. 13-14. Don't let your Sims stand up while they eat, or their comfort will go down.

Hygiene Is Your Friend

Hygiene is especially important on vacation. Your
Sims can get Montezuma's Revenge (*baaaaad* food
poisoning) if they eat while their hygiene is low!
Your Sims will be downright miserable for 10–14
hours if you let them contract this nasty disease, so
be vigilant about washing before meals. If your
Sims eat a meal with a hygiene score below –50,
they have a 25 percent chance of coming down
with the illness.

Once stricken, the unfortunate Sims display no
symptoms for a few hours. Suddenly, they'll dance
around holding their drawers, anxious for a
bathroom. You might even hear the special,
unmistakable sound of a Sim getting sick in the
bathroom. Worse yet, sick Sims have a small
chance of having their bladder scores crash
immediately to 0 points at any time, resulting in
the most embarrassing of accidents! This type of
thing is sure to ruin the day and have severe
effects on your vacation score.

Fig. 13-15. Don't let a sick Sim get more than a dozen steps from a bathroom!

Keep up hygiene by showering or bathing your
Sims once a day, and also send them to take a dip
in the pool or a hot tub if their score drops after a
hard day at play. Monitoring hygiene should be an
easy task, and this is one of those cases where an
ounce of prevention is worth a pound of cure.
There is no cure, in fact, for Montezuma's
Revenge. Once your Sim has it, you've just got
to wait it out to its miserable end, up to half a
day later.

Bathroom Breaks

Although the bladder motive is completely
straightforward, you can still apply a little bit of
strategy to your Sims' bathroom breaks. Your Sims'
bladder motives bottom out about 15 Sim-minutes
after a meal, so corral them toward the bathrooms
shortly after hitting the buffet. Also take
advantage of bathroom proximity whenever it's
convenient, so that you don't have to send your
Sims halfway across the lot later on. Plan your pit
stops so that you can have longer sessions in the
sun and snow.

Serving Up the Fun

Fun is served up in huge portions on Vacation Island, and there are plenty of ways for your Sims to get their fill. When you choose activities for your vacationing Sims, pay attention to their individual personalities. Recreation should cater to the personalities of your Sims.

Fig. 13-16. Playful Sims will have a great time catching big air on a rented snowboard.

The various fun-building activities on Vacation Island each appeal to a particular personality more than others. The following table will help you pick the activity that's right for your Sims.

Activity Motives and Effects

ACTIVITIES	PERSONALITY SERVED	EFFECTS
Balloon Pop	Serious	Decreases Energy and Comfort
Battle Forts	Outgoing	Decreases Energy and Comfort
Bow & Arrows	Grouchy	Can Earn 3-6 Tokens
Chicken Toss	Playful	Can Earn 10 Tokens
Clown Squirt	Sloppy	Can Earn 3 Tokens Per Hit
Fishing Pole	Lazy	Decreases Hygiene
Half Pipe	Playful	Decreases Energy and Comfort
Treasure Hunt	Shy	Can Find Money or Souvenirs
Sandcastle Kit	Playful	Adds to Vacation Score
Snowman Kit	Nice	Adds to Vacation Score
Strength O Meter	Neat	Can Earn 6 Tokens, Decreases Energy
Whack-a-Will	Shy	Can Earn 1 Token Per Whack
Volleyball	Active	Decreases Energy

Let your active Sims enjoy the great outdoors with the help of the many new sports objects. Don't forget old standbys like swimming and basketball. Remember that many of the sports objects cause losses to energy, comfort, and hygiene, so plan for this by timing them with your other endeavors. Have full hunger and bladder motives, for example, before engaging in some of the sporting activities, so that your Sim doesn't end up with a high fun motive but dangerously low in all other motives after they're done with their game.

Buried Treasure

Treasure hunting is one of the new features of the *Vacation* expansion. If you are dedicated, you could actually get away with living indefinitely on the island as a "beach bum," financing your Sims' existence with the help of proceeds from treasures recovered while treasure hunting and fishing. This lifestyle is far more viable if you also have *Hot Date* installed, which allows you to find the diamond necklace and engagement ring, as well.

NOTE

If an adult Sim is aided by a child from the same household while fishing or treasure hunting, they might share a special moment together. Occasionally, the child can help the adult uncover a find with the metal detector, or the adult helps the child use the fishing pole.

Treasure hunting isn't easy, and you have to spend a lot of time doing it to find things of any value. For each hour of time spent metal detecting or fishing, your Sim has a 20 percent chance of finding something. Even so, there's an 80 percent chance that it'll be junk. Every so often, however, it is something of value. A random treasure is generated for your Sim. It can be a souvenir, the pirate's chest (with anywhere from 500 to 1,500 Simoleans inside), or an item of monetary value.

Fig. 13-17. Treasure hunting can actually support a lifestyle of permanent vacation.

Social Butterflies

Social needs are easily served on the island, with many social object interactions available and even more NPC Sims to share them. Your Sims have more fun with higher numbers of participants in anything they do. Volleyball, snowman and sandcastle building, and several other activities all are more fun and more successful with greater numbers of Sims playing.

Two new social activities are introduced in *Vacation*, similar to the additions made in *Hot Date*. You can take your Sims for a dip in the hot tub with new romantic interactions, and you can treat your Sims to some mood-enhancing beverages at the bar. Both of these activities are for adults only, so cover the kiddies' eyes when you go hot tubbing or bar hopping.

Gettin' Steamy in the Hot Tub

The hot tub is your ticket to vacation romance, with several spicy interactions for adult Sims. The Play interaction has the greatest potential relationship and mood payoff, but also it carries a very steep rejection penalty. Before you try this move, make sure your partner is in a very good mood, likes your Sim a lot, and is also naturally playful.

Fig. 13-18. Things can get very steamy in the hot tub.

Wash also requires a good relationship, but it caters to more serious Sims, with a slightly lower payoff. If your Sims are new to the bath and each other, stick to Cuddling and Kissing. Note that Sims will exit the hot tub as soon as they have had their fill of either fun or comfort, so don't take a bath with a Sim who's already enjoying high values in these motives.

Hot Tub Interaction Results

INTERACTION	RESPONSE	DAILY RELATIONSHIP CHANGE	LIFETIME RELATIONSHIP CHANGE	SOCIAL SCORE CHANGE	FUN CHANGE
Cuddle	Accept	2	1	4	4
Cuddle	Reject	-4	-1	0	0
Play	Accept	4	2	8	6
Play	Reject	-6	-4	0	0
Play	Be Accepted	4	2	8	8
Play	Be Rejected	-6	-3	0	0
Wash	Accept	4	1	10	3
Wash	Reject	-10	0	0	0
Wash	Be Accepted	3	0	7	3
Wash	Be Rejected	-7	0	0	0

Tasty Beverages

Bars provide your adult Sims with some excellent opportunities for fun, socialization, and relationship-building. Enjoying drinks from the barmaid in the comfort of dining chairs around a table is best. While seated, your Sims save some precious energy while boosting their comfort scores. Also, you can often get faster service from the barmaid than you can in the crowds at the bar itself.

Fig. 13-19. Bar tables offer your Sims multiple motive satisfaction, making them a better choice than stools or standing.

When your Sims are seated, click on the nearest barmaid to order drinks. The barmaid comes over to take your order. You can talk about interests as you wait for your drinks. Eventually, the barmaid returns with drinks in hand, and the fun begins.

The drinks at the bar are so darn good, they put your Sims in a better mood. Each time Sims take a sip, their relationship requirements for every single interaction drop by one point. After a half dozen sips, a kiss that used to require a relationship of 30 will now be accepted with a just-got-to-know-you score of 24.

Fig. 13-20. Relaxing at the bar is a great way to improve your adult Sims' moods and relationships.

The promiscuity wears off after a little while, but the relationship changes do not. If you're in the mood for more forward interactions than your relationships allow, break the ice with a few tasty beverages, and watch the soggy romance blossom. A session at the bar can be a turning point in a relationship between two Sims who don't share the same interests or personalities. The lowered relationship requirements open up some high-return interactions, allowing the couple to get "over the hump" so that their relationship will support those interactions without the aid of tasty libations.

Fond Memories

All good things must eventually come to an end, and so too must your Sims' vacation. The two most important limiting factors for the extent of your vacation are money and personal relationships. The impact of these factors can be minimized (or even negated) with a few sound vacation strategies, but ultimately you'll probably want to remind your Sims what their home looks like.

> **TIP** There's no way to peek at your vacation score, but the formula provided in this chapter can help you estimate it. A family with two adults and two children would take five days of good-mood vacationing to earn a super souvenir without engaging in any extra point-earning activities. Try keeping loose track of your score, and wait until you've earned your 150 points before departing the island.

While you're on vacation, your Sims won't be going to work and thus won't have their steady income. Meanwhile, most of the things your Sims do on Vacation Island cost money. You can help stanch the financial bleeding by engaging in free or low-cost activities, but you'll still be in the red at the end of the day. If you want to earn money without leaving the island, you'll have to assign some of your Sims to full-time metal detection in the hopes of digging up some treasure chests and lost caches of cash.

Relationships back home are the other compelling reason to end your vacation. While you're away, your Sims' friendships decay at the regular daily rate. You can keep this decay down by purchasing postcards in the gift shop and mailing them to your friends and loved ones back home. Click on the mailbox to send one of these "wish you were here" notes, and you'll enjoy a little boost to your daily relationship score.

Fig. 13-21. Sending postcards is the only way to maintain your relationships back home while your Sims are on vacation.

When your Sims arrive home, they immediately seek to place any souvenirs they've acquired in a display case. If none is available, they place them on any available surface. You can sell unwanted souvenirs for a small profit to recoup the costs of the vacation. After your family has settled in, serve their motive needs and make sure they are ready for work and school in the morning, when they'll be resigned to their daily routine again until their next dream vacation becomes a reality!

When you're ready to say good-bye to paradise, have an adult Sim use the telephone booth to call for a ride home. A vacation shuttle will come and pick up your family for a ride down to the harbor, and you'll be homeward bound. If you think your Sims are in the running for a super souvenir, be sure to depart from the type of lot that corresponds to the super souvenir you want: mountains for the snow globe, woods for the pine cone, and beach for the sun.

Fig. 13-22. All that vacationing can drain the bank in a hurry, so your Sims have to head back to work before they can fund another vacation.

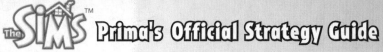